Contents

Introduction 5

Chronology 9

Artist into Designer 1910–1939 13

Design Research Unit 1939–1951 29

International Recognition 1952–1964 50

Rationalisation 1964–1977 86

Bibliography 107

Misha Black in his office, October, 1969.

VICKERS

Misha Black

AVRIL BLAKE
The Design Council

Misha Black

First edition published in the United Kingdom
1984 by The Design Council, 28 Haymarket
London SW1Y 4SU

Printed and bound in the United Kingdom by
The Whitefriars Press Ltd

British Library CIP Data

Blake, Avril
    Misha Black.
    1. Design, Industrial—Great Britain—
    History—20th century
    I. Title
    745.2'0941   TS57

ISBN 0-85072-152 0

Introduction

The great advantage for Misha Black's generation of young designers was the belief that a fundamental truth was beginning to find popular expression in the Modern Movement. 'Truth to materials', 'form follows function', clean lines, clear colours, were ideas expressed by the Bauhaus and brought to a wide audience in the Festival of Britain.

The present generation's desolation in finding only yet another century of fashionable styles was then unknown. Caught up in the new fervour, initiates had only to convince the blind, resistant establishment (a delightful target) and all would be well.

Misha Black, a journalist and lecturer as well as a designer, even in youth preached the gospel of the Modern Movement and made its tenets practical in the commercial world of exhibition design.

Year by year, writing, lecturing, teaching, through his work for the Society of Industrial Artists and Designers, The Design Council, The International Council of Societies of Industrial Design, at the Royal College of Art, giving lectures all over the world, he became spokesman for design – a visual art and therefore not always the most clearly articulate of professions. But Misha Black was clear. Always logical, rational and practical, he argued truth and a depth of thought out of colleagues, students and lecturers at international conferences. He prised criteria from clients. He refused to settle for less than the fundamental truth that had been the promise in his youth.

Perhaps it is the mark of a great man that he seems to have the ability to command immediate attention. Misha had this ability. Whether it was at an international conference or at a meeting or in ordinary casual conversation, he commanded attention. Not by ranting. Not by display. He was mild. He was gentle. He was amusing: but everyone stopped and listened when he spoke and delighted to go on listening.

Throughout his life he embraced new ideas and new developments in a continuing expansion of a philosophy about design. He was able to bring together and to embrace new ideas with a depth of perception that was almost unique. Nothing was taboo in Misha's thinking. Everything had its place and had its connection with what had gone before and what was likely to happen in the future. This ability to see everything in its wider context proved invaluable when, very much in later life, he turned to teaching.

He was, however, more of a diplomat than a philosopher intent on expounding personal views. He was never an advocate for a particular approach or attitude and he never pushed his own personal ideas. He always tried to draw his conclusions from his awareness of wide contexts. He made design the focus of social and economic thinking at any one time.

Even when he had become internationally famous, he remained extraordinarily approachable. Although he became arguably the most outstanding personality of his time in the field of design, he would pay as much attention to a young designer seeking his advice as he would to the captains of industry or the leaders in the educational world. He never sought to confound his audience with a display of learning. He always expressed himself in the simplest possible terms.

He was very much a synthesist, rather than an analyst. He put things together rather than taking them apart. He gave meaning and unity to what, superficially, might be seen as conflicting ideas and events.

When technology outstripped 'truth to materials' and engineering became the anchorman of design for products outside the craft-based industries, Misha Black explored the relevance of engineering to design and advocated changes to be made, accordingly, in design education. His writing on this subject was among his greatest work. Only one short extract, however, is in this book (see page 94). More can be found in the Misha Black archive at the Victoria & Albert Museum.

In this book the author has tried to create an image of the private character of a man who rose from a limited, though good, education and life in the East End of London to become a knight, the head of one of the best-known international design practices, a leader for his profession and a professor at the Royal College of Art. Diaries have been quoted to demonstrate the bright, professional, omnivorous vision. An article he wrote for *Punch* demonstrates his sense of humour (see page 86).

Although Misha Black's many facets and activities have led different people to see him in different lights, his own view of himself seems to have been that of an artist *manqué* and his library was full of gallery and art exhibition catalogues collected at, it seemed, almost every show in London.

In an article entitled 'Design Needs Art', he wrote:

'Over the past fifteen years I have oscillated, like an erratic weathercock, from the view that industrial design is a problem-solving activity owing allegiance only to engineering, to the opinion that its linkage with the fine arts is as important as its dependence on technology.'

He concluded:

'The speciality of the industrial designer is aesthetics: his technical training and experience are the essential armature for giving form to the utilitarian and symbolic needs of mankind. His education must be a springboard for later mature, humane, aesthetic judgement and this postulates an early synthesis of art, technology and social understanding which traditional engineering training only rarely provides.'

One quality of greatness in Misha Black seemed to lie in the fact that he not only spoke well and to the point, he also listened. People have remembered how he would sit through a whole meeting not saying anything, seeming half asleep, and then, at the end, not only summed up the essential truth in what everyone had said but immediately produced an excellent compromise or creative solution.

He was similarly able to document the larger movements in contemporary design with lucid commonsense. When, in the early 1960s, the bright frivolity of Carnaby Street caused something of a design revolution in Britain, challenging the puritanical aesthetic values of the Modern Movement, Black wrote calmly, in an article entitled 'Design Today':

'Design, in common with all other creative activity, is a constantly changing reflection of the life of the whole community. Its avant-garde head is well separated from its distant tail, and the difficulty of any accurate appraisal is that we are always so close to our current design problems as to make it difficult to be certain whether it is an eager head, the solid stomach, or the mangey tail which is within our vision ...'

After the student revolution in the art schools in the late 1960s, which evoked the National Advisory Council on Art Education/National Council for Diplomas in Art and Design Joint Committee Report, he summed up the effects by saying:

'... three fundamental changes had occurred. Firstly the aristocratic concept of the fine arts had been disturbed by the emergence of art forms which were by description "popular", by the young artists' wish to produce an art in which 20th century man could participate and which was not restricted to a self-appointed elite of aesthetes. Secondly, those industries which had been based on craft techniques, such as textiles, ceramics and furniture became progressively automated and demanded technical knowledge and skills from their designers which were not satisfied by the craftsman's personal inventiveness and manual dexterity.

'Thirdly, instructions in industrial design (engineering) had become a new element in design education .... University education based on visual/audio insight and sensibility could prepare young men and women for a role in society which is now largely neglected. The disciplines of art and design could provide the framework for education which does not sacrifice the senses at the altar of the intellect.

'These graduates would not expect to become professional artists or designers; they would be prepared to work as managers and organisers, as entrepreneurs and civil servants, but they might well, in fact, become the supra-artists, not dedicated to the canalisation of their talents and understanding within the confiines of specialisation but able to bring an artist's insight and sensitivity to focus on problems of human relations and the human environment.'

Predicting, in the 1970s, 'The Relevance of Industrial Design in the 1980s' he said

'The period of enthusiasm and self-confidence is ended. Few designers now believe that they can change the world by the excellence of their work. Even if they are comforted by the conviction that their activity influences the environment and is thus an aspect of the external forces which affect social development, they know that they are part of political and economic systems which permit execrable social conditions which are tolerated only because they are a fractional improvement on the past.

'I have started this paper with these seemingly pessimistic words because they describe the present attitude of mind of many designers and which is more usual than exceptional in the minds of design students. But pessimism destroys the capacity for action. Design without conviction ensures mediocrity. It is possible to be a painter or, conceivably, a musician while imbued with unrelieved *Weltschmerz*, but it is not possible effectively to design a city or a chair without at least momentary belief in their validity.

'We must accept our disillusion and the more acute disillusion of the younger designers and yet not allow it to turn into sour pessimism if we are to re-create foundations for the continuation of design and the education of designers into the 1980s. The theories of the Bauhaus are now only partially valid; the sales-oriented creed of the American industrial designers of the 1930s has lost its sales appeal. The civilising influence of Scandinavia is challenged by the extravagant exuberance of Italian designers; Olivetti is suspect and IBM no longer commands uncritical respect. It is significant that, at the Assembly of the International Council of Societies of Industrial Design (ICSID) at Barcelona in October last year it was unanimously agreed that it is no longer necessary to include a definition of industrial design in its constitution; what was implied, but not stated, is that the 54 societies and councils from 33 countries which constitute ICSID cannot agree on what industrial design is. But if the activity cannot be defined, it cannot be practised except as a blind probing towards an instinctively apprehended but shadowy goal....'

Misha Black himself had defined industrial design for ICSID. He had also written the first constitution, based on that of the Society of Industrial Artists and Designers. Working with Count Sigvard Bernadotte, Peter Müller-Munk and Pierre Vago (who became Secretary) Misha Black did the spade work, in 1957, to organise the international body and the first assembly, arranged in Stockholm. Misha Black himself was Vice President from 1957 to 1959 and President from 1959 to

1961. He continued to work for the organisation, still writing letters in bed just before he died in 1977.

ICSID has said, about designers,

'Everything that is made by man is designed, and everything he designs takes on an economic, social and environmental meaning. The quality of life, the use of resources, and the material well-being of man's societies are closely linked to the ability to create man-made products and environments. As never before, design is a critical part of meeting the challenges of human need, rapid change and economic aspirations.'

The pace becomes more and more rapid, the variety of human needs more diverse. The challenge now was summed up by Misha Black in a lecture entitled 'The creation of environment':

'...to influence the environment outside our own homes, collaboration with our neighbours is essential, the formation of civic societies and pressure groups are necessary. It requires political action on a street, neighbourhood or district basis. This is tiresome and time consuming but the fruit of this endeavour can be an environment which is beneficial to our human development instead of harmful to it; it requires the seeing eye of which I have spoken. It can produce what John Donne has called "a knowing joy".'

Avril Blake
Maplehurst
February 1983

Chronology

Born Baku, Russia 16 October 1910
Brought to England 1912
British citizen
Educated: The Dame Alice Owen School

Honours and Professional Qualifications

1932	Member, Society of Industrial Artists
1939	Member, Institute of Registered Architects (MInstRA)
1945	Officer of the Order of the British Empire (OBE)
	Fellow of Society of Industrial Artists (FSIA)
1956/7	President of Society of Industrial Artists
1957	Royal Designer for Industry (RDI)
1965	Medal of the Society of Industrial Artists and Designers
1968	Honorary Doctor of Royal College of Art (HonDrRCA)
1969	Companion of the Institute of Mechanical Engineers
1972	Knight Bachelor
1974/5	Master of the Faculty of Royal Designers for Industry (RDI)
1975	Honorary Doctor of Technology (University of Bradford) (HonDTech)
1975	Professor Emeritus Royal College of Art

Public Appointments

1934–40	Chairman, Artists International Association
1938–50	Member, MARS Group (British section CIAM)
1942–59	Member, Advisory Council, Society for Education in Art
1945	Member, Visual Arts Enquiry, PEP
1948	Chairman, Committee to report on Graphic School of Royal College of Art
1951–67	Member, Advisory Council, Institute of Contemporary Art
1952–54	Member, National Council, Design in Industry Association (President 1975/6)
1954–56	President, Society of Industrial Artists and Designers (Council member 1938–52, 1956–57)
1955–64	Council Member of Council of Industrial Design
1957–64	Member, International Jury for Triennale (Milan)
1958	Member, International Jury for Signe d'Or (Belgium)
1959–61	President of International Council of Societies of Industrial Design (Member, Executive Board 1957–65, Chairman, Education Commission 1965–69)
1959–75	Professor of Industrial Design, Royal College of Art

1959–72	Member, National Advisory Council on Art Education
1964	Member, Jury for La Rinascente Compasso d'Oro (Milan)
1964	Chairman, 1st ICSID/UNESCO Seminar on Industrial Design Education, Bruges, Belgium
	Chairman, 2nd ICSID Seminar, Ulm, W. Germany (1965)
	Chairman, 3rd ICSID Seminar, Syracuse, USA (1967)
1965	Vice President of the Modular Society
1965	Section Chairman, Second Steel Utilisation Congress, Luxembourg
1966–77	Member, Advisory Council to Science Museum
1967–77	Honorary Vice President, National Union of Students
1968–71	Member, Management Committee, Science of Science Foundation
1968–77	Trustee of British Museum
1968	Delegate to 4th ICSID Seminar on Industrial Design Education, Buenos Aires, Argentina
1969–77	Member, Culture Advisory Committee to United Kingdom Commission for UNESCO (Chairman 1973–75)
1969–73	Member, Council of the Newcastle-upon-Tyne Polytechnic
1970	Member, International Jury for Delta d'Oro, Barcelona
1971	Consultant to Indian Institute of Technology, Delhi
1971	Member, Engineering Design Advisory Committee, Council of Industrial Design
1973–77	Member, Scientific Advisory Committee Experimental Cartography Unit (NERC)
1973–77	Master of the Faculty of Royal Designers for Industry

Professional Appointments

1929	Designer, Rio-Tinto Pavilion, Spanish-American Exhibition, Seville
1933–39	Partner, Industrial Design Partnership
1936–50	Architect to Kardomah Ltd (originally Liverpool and China Tea Co Ltd)
1936–38	Design Consultant to Gas Light & Coke Company
1937	Joint Designer, Interior Peace Pavilion, International Exhibition, Paris
1938	Interior Designer, Steel, Coal, Shipbuilding and Public Welfare Halls, United Kingdom Pavilion, Empire Exhibition, Glasgow
1938	Co-ordinator, MARS Exhibition of Modern Architecture, London
1939	Designer, Public Welfare and Maritime Halls, British Pavilion, World's Fair, New York
1940–45	Principal Exhibition Architect to the Ministry of Information
1945–77	Founder Partner, Design Research Unit
1945–48	Industrial Design Consultant to the Tea Bureau
1946	Designer, 'The Birth of an Egg-Cup' section, Britain Can Make It exhibition
1947–53	Designer to UNESCO for Exhibitions in Mexico and Israel

Chronology

1948–51	Member, Presentation Panel and Design Group, Festival of Britain
	Co-ordinating Architect, Upstream Section, South Bank Exhibition
	Architect, Regatta Restaurant
	Co-ordinating Display Designer, Dome of Discovery
1948	Designer, Darkness into Daylight exhibition, Science Museum
1951–55	Design Consultant to BOAC for interior of their headquarters building and maintenance base, London Airport
1952	Consultant to Government of Ceylon for Colombo Exhibition and architect for UK Pavilion
1953	Architect, UK Pavilion, Rhodes Centenary Exhibition, Bulawayo, Southern Rhodesia
1956–62	Design Consultant to British Railways Board for diesel and electric locomotives
1957–60	Co-ordinating Designer for the public rooms in the P&O Orient Liner Oriana
1957–61	Architect to Furniture Exhibition
1959–60	Architect to Civic Trust for rehabilitation schemes at Norwich and Burslem
1960–63	Industrial Design Consultant to Beagle Aircraft
1963–71	Partner, Black Bayes Gibson & Partners
1964–68	Design Consultant to London Transport Executive
1964–77	Design commissions for *The Times,* British Olivetti, Barclay's Bank, Chase Manhattan Bank, British Airports Authority, Co-operative Insurance Society, Alliance Building Society, BP, Kleinwort Benson, British Steel Corporation, Sir Max Rayne, Williams & Glyn's Bank
1965–70	Design Consultant to South Wales Switchgear Limited
1966–67	Consultant Designer to the Ontario Government for their pavilion at International Exhibition, Montreal, Canada
1967	Architect to the Zoological Society for the Small Mammal House (London Zoo)
1967	Industrial Design Consultant to Mather and Platt Ltd
1968–71	Design Consultant to Vickers Ltd
1969–77	Architect and Industrial Designer for Hong Kong Rapid Transit Railway
1969	Designer, Synagogue on Cunard liner Queen Elizabeth 2
1972	Design Consultant to Westminster City Council for Piccadilly Circus redevelopment

(Top) Misha, Sam, their mother and Max Black, 1917.

(Above right) Misha and Max Black, 1914.

(Above) The Blacks and friends, c 1922. Back row, Lionel Black, Mrs Zukerman, Sophia Black and William Zukerman. Front row, Misha, Max, Zuberna Zukerman and Sam.

(Right) Misha (on the left), Max (on the right) and Sam Black (in front of them) c 1923 or '24.

Artist into Designer 1910–1939

Born in Russia on 16 October, 1910, Misha was the second son of Lionel Tcherny, merchant, and Sophia Tcherny, née Divinskaia, who brought him to Britain at the age of 18 months. The family changed their name to Black (the English translation of Tcherny) by deed poll. Misha had an elder brother, Max (born in 1909), a younger sister, Rivka, born in 1920 (who died of cancer about 1960) and a younger brother, Sam, born in 1915.

Misha Black wrote an article for ARK magazine in 1971 describing, his schooling and ambitions:

'When I was a boy at school the only thing I was good at was *art*. This consisted of designing wallpaper patterns which were bowdlerised versions of William Morris reproductions, varied by an occasional textile or dinner plate … As my teachers were puzzled by my ineptitude in all other subjects (willing to learn though I clearly was) they initiated a prize for art when I left school so that I would have at least one success to alleviate my cheerless adolescence … As I

Misha Black (the baby), his father, his mother and his brother Max just before coming to England in 1912.

moved through a fog of imperception towards adulthood, only one thing was clear, at some point I would emerge from somnambulistic youth to become an *artist*. My ambition was modest, there seemed to me then little if any difference between *art* and *commercial art*, while the latter had at least the implication that through it I might avoid malnutrition.

(Left) Crosse and Blackwell exhibition stand by Misha Black, 1928.

(Below) Exhibition stand for Keiller by Misha Black, 1928.

'I was inhibited by an incapacity to draw accurately, so I trollied bales of silk to East End dressmakers and sold made-to-measure enamelled table tops to hygienic house-wives. I spent anxious evenings at the Central School drawing the big toe of Greek casts and the plaster breasts of sexless goddesses, dreaming of the day when I might earn £3 a week in a few hours a day and be free to devote myself to the image of *art* which I only barely comprehended and in the practice of which I was clearly incompetent.'

At 17 Misha Black began to design posters and exhibition stands, mainly for the agent J. Arundell-Clarke. In 1928 he designed a stand for the Rio Tinto Company's display at the Seville Exhibition and went to Spain to supervise the work. On the way home his employers allowed him to stay in Paris for several months to study *art*. Black wrote later that he found, in Paris:

'that I could draw if I was concerned not with stylistic preconception or attempts to memorise but was willing to achieve complete identity with the model or object I was examining with trance-inducing concentration.

'I returned from Paris with 400 drawings and the conviction that Commercial Art could only serve as a stomach filler while I reserved my energies for *art* which I accepted with masochistic dedication as my destiny ... This is a far cry from my present occupation of designing diesel locomotives and underground stations ....'

He returned to England to design more exhibition stands – for Cerebos, for Toblerone, for the Standard Motor Company, for Kelvinator, for Keiller, for Industrial Rotherham, for Esso and for Bainbridge Brothers. All these stands demonstrated Black's skill not only in designing with all the practical needs in mind but, in doing so, for holding

to the great ideal of young designers at this time to find a new simplicity of line and form, to eliminate both ornament and pomposity and to prove that high aesthetic standards could make sound commercial sense.

At this time he met Lucy Rossetti, now Mrs Lucy O'Conor. She was the great niece of Dante Gabriel Rossetti and the grand-daughter of Ford Maddox Brown. She met Misha Black through answering an advertisement in *The Times* which invited 'anybody interested in learning shop-window dressing'

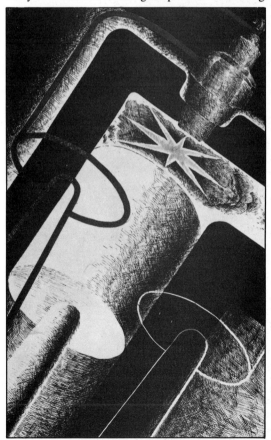

Drawing for a poster by Misha Black, 1928.

Two posters designed by Misha Black for Shell, c. 1928.

to come and do so. Lucy, overawed by her family's painting achievements, felt that her own talent was only sufficient to qualify her as a commercial artist and answered the advertisement which led to classes under a Mr Hans Kiesewetter and work (mainly unpaid) for Messrs Wickhams and Arundell Display Ltd. Misha Black also attended these classes and he and Lucy Rossetti often worked together on window displays.

One display Mrs O'Conor can remember involved a row of hot water bottles which Misha pinned up in a most distinctive pattern.

'Do you like that?' he asked Lucy. She said she did, very much. 'But how have you made them stay up there?' Then Misha realised he had pierced all the bottles, making them useless.

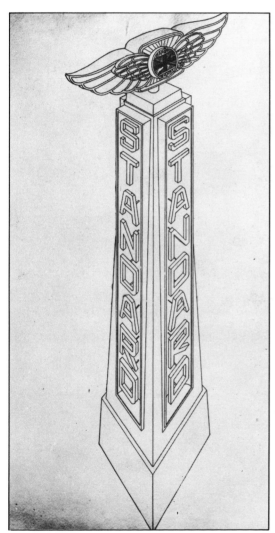

(Above) Illuminated sign in stainless steel designed by Misha Black for the Standard Motor Co. Ltd, c. 1928.

(Above right) Painting of Misha Black by Lucy Rossetti, 1930.

However, other designs were more successful and, in 1930, he suggested to Lucy that they would make more money if they worked for themselves. They decided to call themselves Studio Z and soon found two rooms and a lavatory for a modest weekly rent in Seven Dials. Misha used to sleep at the studio as well as work there. Lucy lived with an aunt. They worked long hours. This was the time of the slump and work was hard to get but they designed bookplates, letter headings, window displays, exhibition stands and a bedside table. The partnership lasted about a year until Lucy, working too hard, fell ill and had to retire from the business. Misha worked on alone until 1933 when he joined Bassett Gray, the forerunner of Industrial Design Partnership and Design Research

Misha Black when he set up Studio Z aged 20.

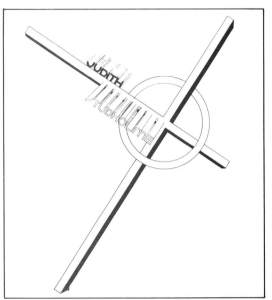

Letter heading by Misha Black for Studio Z.

Display designed for Imperial Airways, c 1930.

Unit. This group had first been established in 1922, with Milner Gray and Charles and Henry Bassett as its partners. The group included:

Chairman: Milner Gray FSIAD		1921–35
Jesse Collins FSIAD	1923–28,	1933–35
E. B. Hoyton RS		1925–35
Associates:		
Paul Drury RE		1925–35
Clive Gardiner		1933–35
Rowland Hilder		1933–35
Graham Sutherland		1928–33

Misha Black joined them in 1933 and continued in the re-formed group, Industrial Design Partnership. IDP began in 1935 and was dissolved in 1940.

(Left) Poster for Cochran's Revue, 1930.

(Below) Card advertising Bassett Gray. Graham Sutherland is among the names of associates.

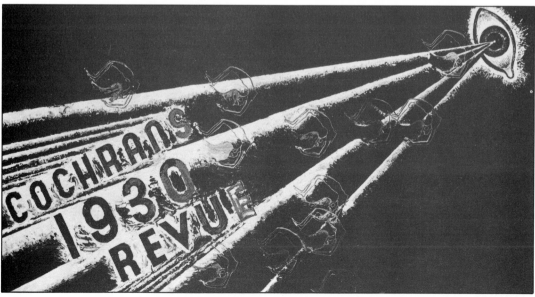

Advertisement for Lyons Corner Houses by Misha Black, 1931.

Letter heading for Industrial Design Partnership by Misha Black.

It included:

Partners:

Milner Gray	1935–40
Misha Black	1935–40
Thomas Gray	1935–40
Jesse Collins	1935–40
James de Holden Stone	1935–40

Associates:

Kenneth Bayes FRIBA FSIAD	1936–40
Paul Drury	1935–40
Clive Gardiner	1935–40
E. B. Hoyton RS	1935–40
Rowland Hilder	1935–40
John Mansbridge	1935–40

Although much of the work carried out by Industrial Design Partnership continued to be in exhibition design, and also in graphics and packaging – for which Milner Gray had earned a considerable reputation – industry was showing an increasing interest in product design and Misha Black designed radios and a television cabinet for E. K. Cole Ltd and the 'Vek' heater for the Gas, Light & Coke Company. These products seem scarcely to have dated. They might well still be marketable today.

He continued to design exhibition stands, however, and one at this period achieved a more than usually notable success – a portable stand for Cooper, MacDougall and Robertson Ltd of Newcastle of which the magazine *Shelf Appeal* wrote at the time (August 1935) 'Shepherds, farmers and "The County" fell for Misha Black's new portable exhibit ...'

Misha began to write articles for *Shelf Appeal* and other magazines showing the same clarity and common sense in his writing that was visible in his designs. 'Displays Displayed' and 'Travelling for Profit' were among the articles written for *Shelf Appeal*: while 'Does your window earn its keep?' and 'A display department which is run – not just allowed to amble' were written for the *Textile Distributor*.

Summing them all up, he wrote an address to the Architectural Association entitled 'Propaganda in Three Dimensions'. In this he described the essential skill of an exhibition designer which should be, he said, that of 'creating an atmosphere':

'Asked to design an exhibition pavilion, the designer should not ask himself how can I make the most efficient use of the site, how can I achieve the most pleasurable forms, how can I create a building which can be run efficiently, which sits naturally in its surroundings, and firmly on its foundation. He may be able to include these admirable desiderata but he might alternatively have to design a building which startles or terrifies the spectator, which astonishes him by its originality, overwhelms him with a sense of its oppressive power or which coerces him by a more delicate approach. In fact easily the most successful building at the New York World's Fair was a monstrous fungoid growth which looked more like a dark grey stone meringue than anything else.

'The approach to the problem is very different from that which normally faces the architect. The primary questions the exhibition designer asks himself must be: what is the psychological effect I wish to create, what is the story I wish to tell, what is the best way of

getting it across to the section of the public which I have been commissioned to influence? If the answer should be mock baronial Tudor, then the exhibition architect, if he faces up to his problem honestly, must design a mock baronial building. He is much more in the position of a stage designer who has to design a set to create a given atmosphere than that of an architect who has been chosen to design a house because that architect's general style happened to be admired by the client.'

He went on to say:

'To know how to achieve these results is to know how to conduct propaganda and to know how to achieve these results by the use of exhibitions is to know how to conduct propaganda in three dimensions.

'It is impossible to separate the architectural and propagandist function of the exhibition designer and unless the designer is in complete sympathy with the propagandist attitude to the problem he will be able only to produce an unsatisfactory compromise which wastes good timber and labour and does no more than confuse the public.

'The architect designing a house must synthesise the practical considerations of accommodation, services, price and other technical requirements into an organic aesthetic whole. The exhibition designer has similar practical considerations to cope with, but he has also the "story" of the exhibition to tell and, if this is lost in the brilliance of the general conception or the ingenuity of the display devices, then the designer is incompetent even if he creates a show which is the main topic of conversation in every architect's office.'

A "Pay Your Taxes" exhibition

'I think the problem can be most easily understood if I try and outline a typical, although non-existing exhibition. I shall deal with a specific war exhibition, although the same kind of approach would be equally suitable for more normal conditions.

'It has, for example, been agreed that a campaign to make people pay their income tax promptly and cheerfully is necessary. The main lines of the campaign will have been decided and the exhibition designer is asked if he thinks that this is a subject which can be translated into three dimensional form and satisfactorily presented to the public through that medium.

'The reply in this particular case might be that it could be done if the exhibition was on a reasonably large scale and if enough money could be spent on it to make the subject sufficiently exciting to entice people to visit it.

'The exhibition designer has a particular problem, different from that of other propagandists. The advertisement in the daily paper is before the reader at every breakfast table and need only be sufficiently forceful to entice the reader to move his eye-balls slightly from the news column to the advertisement; the propaganda film is usually part of the normal cinema programme and the audience would have to take the positive action of leaving the theatre or closing their eyes if they were to avoid seeing it. Posters directly assault the innocent stroller as he walks down the street. The radio needs only to cajole the listener to turn a knob to enable its message to be heard. But the exhibition designer must usually persuade people to take the direct, positive action of making a special visit to the exhbition, to enter the building and to walk right round the show until the message is absorbed.

'In the income tax example, therefore, the first essential would be a title which, when seen in the Press and poster advertisements,

would excite peoples' curiosity sufficiently to make them come to the exhibition. Something such as "How to pay for the war by easy instalments" might do if it were not so long and clumsy.

'Having got the public there, the first impression would need to be sufficiently unusual to get them to start walking round, instead of just sticking their noses in and beating a hasty retreat at the sight of dull walls filled with drear-looking photographs and statistics. A room full of whirling machinery or machine guns destroying Hitler statuettes by shooting pennies at them might suffice for a first impression.

'The plan and visual emphasis would then need to lead the visitor to an exhibition of model tanks, submarines, battleships, etc, preferably moving models with captions reading: "It costs ... to make a gun," " ... to fire a torpedo", " ... to build a battleship". "And who is to pay for it?" At that stage the snags would become apparent and either the physical impossibility of retreating in his tracks or some exciting new display would be necessary to ginger up the visitor's flagging enthusiasm.

'A note on the amount of tax paid by the Germans or the amount paid by the very rich in this country might then be appropriate. After this the facts of how much the normal person pays would be explained by animated statistics and by the translation of cold figures into some human understandable form, so that they could be understood and remembered even by those people who have never previously paid a direct tax. The advantages of this form of taxation would be stated, how much will be refunded after the the war and what happens to the tax when collected.

'The exhibition might include an automatic lathe which visitors could operate by placing a shilling (provided by the management) into a slot; every time a shilling was inserted a cartridge case would be produced. A further section off the main traffic lanes could explain the general economic problems of the war to the more interested spectators. Finally, there would be a pat on the back for the workers not only producing munitions but also paying for them at the same time and an information bureau for the answering of personal enquiries.

'This is, of course, only a very brief outline of the form such an exhibition could take, but even from this it can be seen how complete a story can be told by an exhibition – how a complete survey can be made of a dull subject which most people might not be willing to study if presented through other media. The visitor coming away from such an exhibitiion would admittedly not rush off immediately to pay his arrears of tax, but he would be more favourably disposed to doing so and might have a clearer picture of why it is essential for him to make these extra sacrifices.'

In this year, 1935, Misha Black married Helen Lilian Evans, daughter of Frank Foster Evans, engineer, by whom he had one son, Jacob, born 1939, and one daughter, Julia, born 1942.

He also became Secretary to the MARS Group, the Modern Architecture Research Group which had been formed at the beginning of the 1930s.

The group had two objectives: firstly, for architects, engineers, allied technicians and others, to meet, with the purpose of furthering an architecture to serve the needs of society; and secondly, to co-operate in furthering and supporting the aims of the National Groups organised in other countries who were associated in the International Congresses for Modern Architecture.

It has been said about the MARS Group that they were not a minor group of modernists but a collection of idealists: architects with *beaux arts* and British School in Rome backgrounds and some with no accepted basic architectural training, as well as engineers, artists and writers. They were encouraged and ably supported by the Architectural Press and, in particular, by H. de Cronin Hastings, J. M. Richards and, above all, by P. Morton Shand, who made important contributions to the *Architectural Review*

The MARS Group was viewed with suspicion by a number of traditional architects but with respect by a few. It was apolitical. It staged an exhibition 'New Homes for All' in Olympia in 1934, displaying the research programme it had carried out on working class housing in Bethnal Green. In January 1938 it staged another exhibition, 'New Architecture', held at the Burlington Galleries, for which Misha Black was co-ordinating designer.

Another important contribution by MARS was the 'London Plan' but that came later. It was the work mainly of Arthur Korn and Felix Samuely. The MARS group undoubtedly changed the course of architecture in this country. It brought architecture and interior design in its fullest sense closer together, accepting that it was impossible to say where architecture ends and interior design begins. Le Corbusier described it as *consisting of men of goodwill and good faith working with enthusiasm and the sensitiveness of artists.'*

Members of the Modern Architecture Research Group were:

Ove Arup
C. R. Ashbee
John Betjeman
M. J. Blanco White
G. M. Boumphrey
Marcel Breuer
B. Carter
Hugh Casson
H. T. Cadbury-Brown
Anthony M. Chitty
George Checkley

Serge Chermayeff
Denis Clarke Hall
Wells Coates
A. D. Connell
G. Dawson
Elizabeth Denby
C. H. De Peyer
L. W. A. T. Drake
Michael Dugdale
J. Earley
Joseph Emberton
Clive Entwistle
F. Digby Firth
Gerald Flower
E. Maxwell Fry
Frederick Gibberd
D. Goddard
Ernö Goldfinger
Walter Goldesmith
Walter Gropius
Val Harding
M. Hartland Thomas
H. de C. Hastings
C. Helsby
W. Holford
E. Kaufmann
W. P. Keen
R. A. Kirby
A. Korn
B. Lubetkin
Colin Lucas
E. W. Mallows
J. L. Martin
Raymond McGrath
L. Moholy-Nagy
Raymond Mortimer
Elizabeth Nagelschmidt
Christopher Nicolson
Colin T. Penn
D. Pleydell-Bouverie
Herbert Read
J. M. Richards

Godfrey Samuel
Felix Samuely
Philip Scholberg
P. Morton Shand
Thomas Sharp
R. H. Sheppard
Hazen Sise
R. T. F. Skinner
G. Stevenson
John Summerson
Cyril Sweett
William Tatton Brown
Ralph Tubbs
W. L. Vinycomb
Basil Ward
J. K. Winser
F. R. S. Yorke
and H. Zweigenthal

Its patrons were The Earl of Derby, Viscount Wakefield, Lord Horder and Sir Michael Sadler.

Other activities for Misha Black included the British anti-war movement and the Artists' International Association of which he had been a founder member in the early 1930s. Henry Moore was also a member of this group.

Misha also worked to build up the Society of Industrial Artists, the first society of its kind in the world, which was begun by Milner Gray and a group of designer friends in 1930. This small band of designers and illustrators 'felt so passionately about the need to improve ourselves and our kind,' Milner Gray has remembered,

'that we decided to band together to form a professional association. So eager were we that we achieved our first goal after only eighteen months of argument and debate ... At the time of these beginnings of our Society, it was laid upon us by the external authority of the Board of Trade that we should not be permitted to become a trade union, and so it is that, by accident and/or design, we lay claim to being a professional association.'

One of Misha Black's earliest jobs with Industrial Design Partnership was to re-design, in collaboration with Walter Landauer, the two Kardomah cafés in Piccadilly and Manchester. These went unchanged until some considerable time after the war and would hold their own in competition with any café design achieved today.

The author, herself, has drunk coffee in the Piccadilly Kardomah, still with the Misha Black interior, after the Second World War. The impression was of comfort and quality, of pains taken in the detailing of the design, of elegant discreet decoration and lighting, and of privacy to talk in a two-bench alcove with tiled table top, Chinese bowl, traditional cruet, neat flat ashtray and little silver bell with which to ring for service.

(Top) The Kardomah Cafe, Piccadilly, 1947.
(Above) The Kardomah Cafe, Birmingham, designed by Misha Black and Walter Landauer.
(Left) Letter heading for The Artists International Association.

The Kardomah Cafe, Knightsbridge.

Jobs in 1937 included a window display for Permutit in collaboration with Jessie Collins. Misha Black also designed book jackets for three books by Anthony Powell and won a headline in the *Advertiser's Weekly* (20 February 1936) 'Misha Black wants *Taste* in Neon'.

The redesign of another Kardomah café, in Cardiff, followed in 1938. Meanwhile Black's exhibition stands included the UK Government Pavilion at the Empire Exhibition in Glasgow. Of this the *Evening Dispatch* wrote: ' ... by general agreement the United Kingdom Pavilion is the finest contribution which His Majesty's Government has ever made to any exhibition.'

There followed a 'Mr Therm' display for the Gas, Light & Coke Company in 1939; a display in

The Empire Exhibition, Glasgow, 1938. Mural by Clive Gardiner. Architect: H. J. Rowse. Display designer: Misha Black.

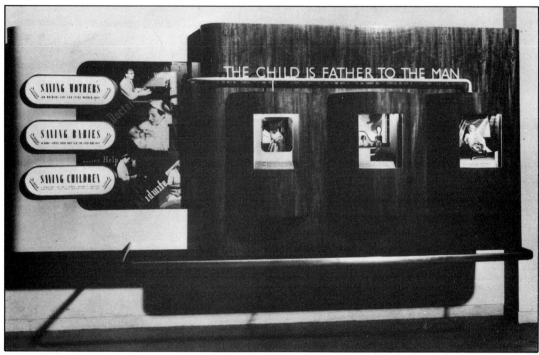

SAVING MOTHERS

SAVING BABIES

SAVING CHILDREN

THE CHILD IS FATHER TO THE MAN

the British Pavilion at the New York World's Trade Fair in 1939; and 'Towards a Fitter Britain' exhibition for the Ministry of Health. In 1939 Black also designed a television cabinet for Ekco Ltd, which was marketed at £100.

Then came the war.

(Above) Social Services Section of the United Kingdom Pavilion, World's Fair, New York, 1939. Designed by Misha Black in association with Thomas Gray and Kenneth Bayes ARIBA, the display dealt with infant and maternity welfare. The three drums on the right each contain four stages; a screen carrying descriptive lettering passes over the proscenium concealing the changing from one stage to another. The photo montage and 'stage sets' were designed by John Barker.
(Left) Misha Black aged 27, 1937.

Design Research Unit 1939–1951

When war was declared Industrial Design Partnership was disbanded. Milner Gray and Misha Black went to work for the Ministry of Information. Misha Black, with his already considerable reputation as an exhibition designer, was made Principal Exhibitions Officer.

The Battle of Britain was then fought and won, but Europe remained Hitler's and the Allies were fighting in North Africa. London was bombed every night. It seemed a strange time to hope, but at least two people went on doing so: Marcus Brumwell, chairman and managing director of Stuart's Advertising Agency and his friend Herbert Read, the distinguished design historian and critic. They sat down to a ration-restricted dinner in a house in Surrey one night in 1942 and began to discuss a plan for forming a group of designers and artists to design a new world after the war. Herbert Read's book *Art and Industry*, published in 1934, had come to be regarded almost as a bible by designers at the time. Now he had the vision to think of a design office on a wider scale than had ever before been conceived.

Stuart's Advertising Agency had banded together during the war with a group of smaller agencies who gave each other mutual support.

Misha Black during the second world war, working for the Ministry of Information. He and his draughtsmen were chiefly concerned with design for aircraft production, but they did give some thought, even then, to the problems which would confront British industry after the war.

Calling themselves the Advertising Service Guild, the group shared resources, including office accommodation for bombed-out members, and together supported and later took over Mass Observation, one of the earliest market research organisations. Brumwell and Read discussed their proposals with Cecil D. Notley who was then head of Notley Advertising, another member of the Guild and, as a result of these discussions, Notley invited Milner Gray to set down on paper a detailed plan for the kind of design service they felt would be needed.

Gray wrote to Notley:

'The purpose of the formation of a group such as is envisaged is to make available immediately a design service equipped to advise on all problems of design, and to form a nucleus group which, through contacts established during the war period with specialist designers and experts in all appropriate fields, would be in a position at the end of the war to expand and undertake the wider services which may then be demanded of it.

'The final aim is to present a service so complete that it could undertake any design case which might confront the State, Municipal Authorities, Industry and Commerce.'

Milner Gray's note went on to describe the organisation of his proposed design group in some detail. It was clearly his suggestion for a three-part structure embracing the functions of design, research and administration which anticipated the title eventually given to the new design group – Design Research Unit.

The Unit was set up on 1 January 1943, and Herbert Read was its first manager and sole member of staff. He installed himself in a small office in Kingsway from which he set out to introduce to potential clients the new service offered by the Unit. The service would be provided by DRU's first team of associates: Milner Gray, Misha Black,

(Above) Field Marshall Montgomery inspecting exhibits at the 1945 British Army Exhibition. On his left are Duff Cooper and General Koenig. On his right stands Misha Black, who directed the design of the exhibition.
(Right) King George VI and Queen Elizabeth open the 'Britain Can Make It' exhibition at the Victoria and Albert Museum, 1946. Misha Black is talking to the King in this photograph.

the architects Frederick Gibberd and Sadie Speight, the structural engineer Felix Samuely and the designer Norbert Dutton, all of whom continued to run their own practices, except Black, Gray and Dutton who were still employed at the Ministry of Information.

Slowly the Unit got under way and by the end of the first year the problem of publicising the service and organising the few commissions that were received required more time than Herbert Read was able to give to it. Early in 1944 DRU advertised for a full-time manager: Bill Vaughan was appointed, and held the fort until the founder partners could be released from their war-time jobs.

Milner Gray designed an exhibition called 'Design at Home' for the Council for the Encouragement of Music and the Arts (later the Arts Council). Misha Black designed the 'MAP Exhibition', 'The Battle for France' exhibition, and the 'British Army' exhibition in Paris. However DRU really went into business in 1946 with the 'Britain Can Make It' exhibition held in September at the Victoria & Albert Museum.

(Above) 'The Birth of an Egg Cup' section of the 'Britain Can Make It' exhibition, Victoria and Albert Museum, London. September 24– December 31, 1946. Designer: Misha Black (Design Research Unit).

(Right) 1946. The giant egg symbolized the theme of a special exhibit at the 'Britain Can Make It' exhibition, designed to illustrate the role of the industrial designer. Even an egg-cup, it was demonstrated, creates marketing, production and other problems which the designer is trained to solve.

PHOTO UNION

Writing of this period, Gordon Russell, who was Director of the then Council of Industrial Design from 1947 to 1959, said:

'industry as a whole was complacently unaware that anything was wrong with the goods it produced. Undeniably it was true that they could all be sold easily at the moment, but the seller's market would pass, competition would greatly increase in the world markets and then suitability and look of the goods – their quality – would become as important as price and delivery.'

The Council tried to teach industry that it needed designers. Misha Black's egg display at the 'Britain Can Make It' exhibition spelt out the message simply and logically. Using a giant egg to attract attention and an egg-cup as his example of product design, he explained how even the simplest mass-produced product creates a multitude of problems which it is the designer's job to solve.

DRU preached the same gospel to industry in a small booklet produced about this time in which partners and associates contributed individual chapters. This read:

'INDUSTRIAL DESIGN. What is it?

'Properly applied to any product, Industrial Design should achieve the following:

'Greater efficiency in use and improved appearance. Therefore greater value to the user or consumer. Increased sales and, in many cases, reduced production costs.

'Industrial design is the intelligent, practical and skilled association of art with industry. It is not the application of decoration as an after-thought, like gilt on the gingerbread or tinsel on the Christmas tree. It certainly is not a quack attempt to disguise a product to look like something else – as, for example, a radio set designed to imitate a Sheraton cabinet.

'Industrial design does not even limit itself – as some imagine – to giving an article

a nice shape or colour, or improved appearance, though this is of course important. Good industrial design is more than this because it takes into account efficiency of manufacture and fitness for purpose. Judging by the thousands of articles produced by the industry of this country there is a need for guidance in design. Too many articles are produced as they are because "they have always been made that way". Too many articles are produced because they work, without any thought for the person who has to work them. Too many articles are produced by people who have only to make them and who never have to live with them.

'If this were not so, why is it difficult to tell at twenty yards whether a taxi is engaged or not? Why do you have to be right in front of a train indicator to be able to tell when the next train goes to Surbiton? Why do sewing machines delight in golden tracery decoration that went out with the hansom cab? Why do we still have to be scalded with steam when we grasp a kettle handle? Why do we still have fringes on lampshades? Why do women get backache merely because they wash up? Why should they wash up? Why does it take hours to clean a car? Why does farm machinery look as if it were designed by the late Heath Robinson?

'The answer to all these questions, and many more, lies in the fact that there has never been a proper marriage between the engineer and the artist. The fault has often been with the artist: "Why doesn't the fellow come down to earth?" "He has ideas but he is not practical." "If only he'd listen to us."

'The fault has often been with the manufacturer: "We've done very well up to now, why should we change?" "That's the way we make it – they can take it or leave it." "No one bothers about the looks of our job – it's the works that matter." "We make machines, not pretty pictures."

'It was to bridge this gap between the manufacturer and the designer and to bring about intelligent co-operation that the Design Research Unit was formed.

'We all know that a well-made, well-finished and attractive looking article is readily sold – whether the cost is a few pennies or hundreds of pounds. The better the article, the better its design, the greater utility to its purchaser. This greater utility may be due to one or more such factors as:

being stronger
being lighter in weight
occupying less space
being easier to keep clean
being cheaper to run
being more accessible for repairs and service
lasting longer

and many other such points in addition to joy of ownership.

'Experience has shown that good industrial design frequently leads to reduction of manufacturing costs by a saving in bulk of materials, by the introduction of alternative and more economical materials, or by the nature of the design resulting in fewer operations with a consequent saving in labour and materials. Furthermore, larger sales turnover almost always leads to a cut in manufacturing costs.'

The booklet went on to answer the question 'Who is the designer?' It explained 'What the designer does', talked about 'New products and new materials', 'The design group idea', 'Why design research?', 'How much does it cost?', 'The value of design in overseas trade' and described 'Some typical jobs already carried out by DRU'.

It was illustrated with a stoneware wine jar and label for the Mid Sussex Canning and Preserving

Company Ltd, designed by Milner Gray; a station unit for the London Passenger Transport Board by Misha Black; door furniture in aluminium by Robert Gutman; a hammock principle armchair for Christie-Tyler Ltd by Milner Gray and Thomas Gray; a tubular steel chair for the Scholl Manufacturing Company Ltd by Norbert Dutton and Ronald Ingles; a ship's binnacle redesigned for Henry Hughes & Son Ltd by Douglas Scott in collaboration with Norbert Dutton; a china tea service for Foley China by Milner Gray; industrial

Stoneware wine jar and label for the Mid-Sussex Canning and Preserving Co Ltd by Milner Gray RDI. This was another illustration in Design Research Unit's booklet 'Industrial Design', 1946.

location planning room for the Ministry of Production by Norbert Dutton; an incubator for
Western Incubators Ltd by Felix Samuely and
Milner Gray; a design for the Ontario Services
Club in Regent Street by Misha Black in association with Bronek Katz; a shop front for Kardomah
by Misha Black; furniture by Robert Gutman; and
the 'Vek' convection heater for the Gas, Light &
Coke Company by Misha Black.

The booklet was an outward and visible sign of
the new form of associateship that was now intro-

*(Above) Station Unit for the London Passenger
Transport Board by Misha Black. This photograph
appeared in Design Research Unit's booklet
'Industrial Design', 1946.*
*(Below right) The Ontario Services Club. Architect:
Misha Black in association with Bronek Katz and
Kenneth Bayes ARIBA, 1943.*

*(Top) Tubular steel chair for the Scholl
Manufacturing Co Ltd, by Norbert Dutton, MSIA
and Ronald Ingles, MSIA. This photograph
appeared in Design Research Unit's booklet
'Industrial Design', 1946.*

duced within the firm. Marcus Brumwell bought up all the shares from the Advertising Service Guild and became the Unit's sole owner, establishing a holding company to control its finances. This change made for much tighter direction of financial policy and offered office space, services and a financial pool to associate members who included Clive Entwistle, Frederick Gibberd, Robert Gutmann, Ronald Ingles, Bronek Katz, Brian Peake, Sadie Speight, George Williams and Gordon Andrews.

Writing about this time in his introduction to *The Misha Black Australian Papers*, Gordon Andrews said:

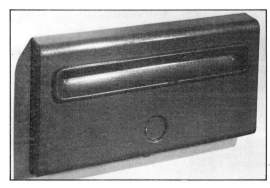

(Above) A meeting of the Design Research Unit Board of associated designers in March, 1948. Back row, left to right, are Marcus Brumwell, Robert Gutmann, Brian Peake and George Williams. Front row, left to right, are Sadie Speight, Frederick Gibberd, Milner Gray, Dorothy Goslett, Bronek Katz, Herbert Read, Misha Black and Clive Entwistle.
(Left) Misha Black's 'Vek' Convection Heater for the Gas, Light & Coke Co.
(Right) The Ceylon Tea Centre, Regent Street, London.

'It was very good – they found work and I did it. This is the way it would work – Misha would go to a meeting with me and the client. We'd thrash all round the problem, what it was all about, and we'd come to some basic decision. We'd come away from the meeting and have further discussions about it and I'd gather all the information that I needed – let's say for an exhibition. I would put something down on paper and when I felt I'd solved the problem that we'd set ourselves, I'd discuss it all with Misha. He'd usually discuss points which he felt might improve it, we'd finally agree and submit it to the client. Always successfully – I can't remember a job that got knocked back.'

Asked about Misha Black's contribution to a design problem, Gordon Andrews said:

I suppose conceptualisation would be the main contribution to any design solution and the capacity to organise and express a situation. Also the ability to extract the essence of the problem from the client, because first of all the client must tell you what it is all about. If he knows! Somewhere or other he knows.

Misha was particularly good at extracting facts from people who didn't know that they knew ....'

Misha himself, in *Group Practice in Design,* put forward the new and original ideas that were already proving so successful in the running of the Design Research Unit:

'Design groups should not be happy families acquiescent to a father-figure leader. They should be disturbed by theoretical differences and opposing creative convictions; their members should be passionate in their criticism of their colleagues' work and hot tempered about their personal rights and dignity. The basis of group organisation is that it is a voluntary assembly of people: no-one is compelled to stay in the group, anyone may leave it at any time. The fact that a group stays in existence is proof of its validity, but its calm outer face must conceal inner conflicts. If its creative working interior also is an undisturbed calm, then it has become as lifeless as a dead Sputnik, still orbiting aimlessly round the world.'

In 1944 Misha Black designed The Tea Centre in Lower Regent Street; the 'Darkness into Daylight' exhibition; the 'Report to the Nation' displays; a Central Office of Information exhibition at Charing Cross and, in 1947, was appointed as co-ordinating architect for the up-stream section of the Festival of Britain. The year before a drawing was published in *The Ambassador* showing a proposal by Misha Black for using the derelict South Bank of the Thames for an international fair. Misha's design for the Festival was another Crystal Palace, more ambitious even than Paxton's. He had a life-long love affair with the 1851 exhibition, wrote about it several times and filled his private home with prints and souvenirs.

The 'Darkness into Daylight' exhibition, held in the Science Museum, South Kensington in 1948.

'Group practice, in its essence, depends on those who are in the group believing that they are within that compass. They must believe that their own contribution to the group is an active factor of its existence, and that for them to leave it would reduce its effectiveness. Their loyalty to the group must be sufficient for them to be as much concerned with its well-being and reputation as with their own personal glory. They must willingly acknowledge that the leadership within the group structure is fairly assumed, not imposed, and capable of being changed if it should deteriorate into ineffectiveness. They must accept that their salaries properly reflect their individual contribution to the group and that when profits are made they are fairly distributed.

'In partial contradiction to these personal beliefs and attitudes, the group, if it is to have any sustainable validity, must be stronger than its parts, and thus able to continue and to grow even if many of those who are its constituent elements leave it. It must be capable of mutation and development irrespective of personalities.

'Many architectural and design offices whose public personae are the names of their originators are group offices innocently disguised, but to come within the orbit of this paper they must exhibit one distinguishing feature: the creative originating work done by the group must be a distributed activity, the office must not be an association of a creative queen bee with draughtsmen executants diligently obeying the royal command. Shared creative responsibility is the basic requirement of group organisation ...

'Design groups are originated in two primary forms: they are assembled by young designers who share the same attitudes and who believe that co-operation is psycho-

Design for the 1951 South Bank Exhibition by Misha Black, drawn by Hilton Wright. This appeared in 'The Ambassador' magazine, no 8, 1946.

logically, socially and organisationally more profitable than personal isolation, or they are groups of designers brought together by external events to achieve a known goal within a relatively short period. The first type of group is open-ended, believing in a limitless future; the second is closed, knowing that its dissolution is predetermined ...

'Personal anonymity has the major advantage of allowing all credit to accrue to the group, so that its reputation grows, undiminished by changes in its personnel or internal structure, but I prefer the system of individual acknowledgement under the group umbrella.

'There is an uncontrollable, if irrational, tendency for those who are outside the group to identify its creative achievements with single individuals irrespective of their real creative contributions. Published personal credits restrict that tendency and simultaneously erect criteria for individual conduct and responsibility within the group itself. In actual working practice the method of apportioning credit may go through tidal phases, from anonymity at the formation of the group, to individual acknowledgement, and then a return to anonymity when the reputation of the group is so high for that to be more important to its members than any personal approbation.

'Idealism is an essential element in group acitivity, but this idealism is related only to the quality of the work produced, to the creative function of the group, to its shared concept of form and its relation to the needs of our society: such creative group idealism does not resolve the anxious cares of private life. Idealism is the essential bone structure of the group, but sentimentality is a disease which will quickly debilitate and finally destroy it ...

The design group for the Festival was led by Sir Hugh Casson, co-ordinating architect for the down-stream section of the Festival. It included James Holland, James Gardiner, Ralph Tubbs and Misha Black. James Holland, Ralph Tubbs and Ralph Freeman worked with Misha Black on the up-stream section. DRU was involved in the design of the interior furnishing for the Dome of Discovery; the Regatta Restaurant (designed by Alexander Gibson who joined the Unit in 1948); and the Bailey bridge for pedestrians across the Thames, beside the Hungerford Bridge.

Strikes and shortages beset the building of the Festival. The first five months of 1951 were the wettest for many years. the Bailey bridge collapsed into the river and had to be fished out and started again. On the night of the 3rd of May, after King George VI had declared from the steps of St Paul's that the Festival was officially open, there were still exhibits waiting to be set up, including some in the Dome of Discovery. The construction workers knocked off at five o'clock that evening, leaving the designers to hump the remaining exhibits into position themselves, working most of the night. All the same, the Dome was finished before the King lead a party of invited guests on a private tour of inspection the following morning.

And the Festival was a success. Only those who had been young throughout the grim years of the war and the even more dull, more deadly 'Age of Austerity' that followed it could fully appreciate quite what the festival of Britain meant to a whole generation of British people.

'London's Gayest Night for Years', reported the headlines in the *Sunday Express* on 6 May, 1951. 'Fairyland at Midnight.' 'Traffic chaos.' 'Packed five deep on Waterloo Bridge, they had a grandstand view of the brilliantly lit South Bank.'

Even Raymond Mortimer, in *The Sunday Times,* rather reluctantly admitted at the end of his lukewarm report:

'It's all such fun and the feeling of enterprise and enthusiasm is infectious – Flying staircases, huge ships, seaside resorts in miniature, tractors ploughing the air, cafés that look like cranes or parachute-schools, dissolving views of geological changes, everywhere there is something fresh and fanciful....'

'The Festival', said Misha Black later,

'spot-lit and gently pushed forward an already existing style (of architecture and design) – it did not create one .... The centralised control resulted in the design concepts throughout the Festival exhibitions being positive and coherent, clearly arising from convictions about technique and from commonly shared views by the architects and designers concerned. It thus had, to the uninitiated, the appearance of a new "style". But it was, in fact, no new system of building. It was not based on any revolutionary design concept or new aesthetic theory .... The Festival triggered off a deep unsuspected need in Britain which, blacked out for too long, was suddenly released by that kind of colour and gaiety for which one must return to Morris dancers and Maypoles for comparison .... The major contribution of the Festival was the support it has given to those who value quality above quantity, worth more than wealth.'

In less austere mood, he wrote in the book *A Tonic to the Nation* published by Thames & Hudson:

'We were very serious. If the South Bank Exhibition was to exude gaiety the architectural clowns who provided it would, themselves, be morosely and professionally dedicated to the task. Those of us who were responsible for the design of the exhibition set ourselves two objectives. The first was to demonstrate the quality of modern architecture and town planning; the second to show that painters and sculptors could work with architects, landscape architects and exhibition designers to produce an aesthetic unity.

'On these two counts our success was complete. We failed to achieve many peripheral objectives and thus dulled the bloom of our basic achievements, but we did produce a contemporary enclave on the South Bank and vanquished (at least for the time being) those who claimed that modern architecture (as we were content to describe it) was unacceptable to the tradition-conscious British and could not be welded satisfactorily into the fabric of an ancient city. The South Bank proved also that informal town planning could give character and a sense of place to a small area, and that majestic avenues were not the only recipe for urban pleasure.

'But this being conceded, as I feel sure it must be by those who visited the exhibition, it remains true that there was little real innovation, almost nothing on the South Bank which had not previously been illustrated in the architectural magazines. Geodesic domes, random stone walling, laminated timber trusses, stretched canvas and glazed facades were already, in 1948, accepted design idioms, the subjects of study and argument in all architectural schools. The Skylon was brand new, the rest was the British issue of international architectural currency, but what had previously been the private pleasure of the *cognoscenti* suddenly, virtually overnight, achieved enthusiastic public acclaim. Architecturally the South Bank exhibition was a milestone; it is sad that many imagined it to be a signpost to be used later to justify the commercial buildings which have more often, over the past quarter century, degraded than improved our cities. But it also set the stage for those architects who could profit from the new climate of perception and acceptance. That architects with the requisite creativity and sensitivity proved to be thin on the ground in the later '50s and '60s was not the fault of the South Bank team; that civic and commercial developers were quicker to accept the fashionable quirks of the exhibition rather than its fundamental concepts was more a saddening social comment than grounds for criticism of Festival architecture.

'But for the moment, the five months' long moment, the air was rich with applause, and only those of us who had been simultaneously fathers and midwives to the South Bank birth were conscious of the ailments of the child who fortunately was destined only for a short, if exuberant, life.

'I shall later adumbrate our basic misconceptions, but let me first describe our one unquestionable success.

'From the earliest planning exercises, the Festival Design Group were determined to celebrate the talents of Britain's artists simultaneously with those of its architects and designers. We sought the collaboration of the famous and those who were not already renowned, and this collaboration was enthusiastically provided. Henry Moore, Jacob Epstein, Barbara Hepworth, Keith Vaughan, Victor Pasmore, Ben Nicholson, John Minton, Felix Topolski, Frank Dobson, Graham Sutherland, John Piper, Reg Butler and some twenty other artists carved, modelled and painted in complete unison with the architects who ensured that walls were available for murals and plinths for sculpture. Practically every concourse was designed to contain a major work; each building was a sanctuary for important works of art.

'It was odd that this raised little comment from the 8½ million visitors or the Press. Only a few years previously Epstein's "Rima" in Hyde Park had been tarred and feathered for reasons which were explicit only to barbarians, but on the South Bank Epstein seemed barely noticed, Hepworth was accepted with a shrug, while the magnificent Henry Moore attracted less attention than the hugh bolders which brought a whiff of Cumberland to the site.

'The reason for this nonchalant reaction was partly *embarras de richesse* .... it is not surprising that a carved block of stone only eight feet high should seem, to most, of little importance when the Skylon soared to the sky and the Dome of Discovery spanned the days of the year. But for those who were willing to shorten their sights, to seek for quality rather than scale, the contribution of the artists was a special pleasure.

'Each of the co-ordinating architects awarded himself one building which he, himself, designed; it was the life-line to sanity – a specific job to compensate for the tasks of co-ordination which demanded diplomacy and

The Bailey Bridge, South Bank Exhibition, 1951. Decorative scheme by Design Research Unit.

persuasion as much as perception. I chose the Regatta Restaurant and the decoration of the Bailey bridge across the Thames. In this South Bank corner my colleague, Alexander Gibson, and I set out to show how a bulding could be a neutral *ambiance* for the work of artists, how vision could be satiated while stomachs were repleted and that practical purpose need not be sacrificed to architectural quality. When visitors approached the restaurant over the Bailey bridge they were assailed by the whirling abstraction of a tiled mural by Victor Pasmore; for the garden Lynn Chadwick built a delicate construct; the lower vestibule was graced by a mural by John

The Regatta Restaurant, South Bank Exhibition, Festival of Britain, 1951.

Tunnard; inside the restaurant by a painting by Laurence Scarfe. The door handles were bronze hands modelled by Mitzi Cunliffe, which Barbara Hepworth refused to touch as she asociated them with amputation. In all it was a visual feast of a higher order than the food, but for myself and a few others it was a private joy which compensated, or at least so I like to believe, for our errors of architectural detail.

'It is regrettable that no careful analysis was made of the failure, in terms of public interest, of the brave attempt to unify art with architecture which characterized the whole South Bank concept. It is probable that the fault resided in our lack of sufficient appreciation of the problem of scale. We, and the artists, were too timid and inexerienced. It may be that we would have done better with fewer and bigger pieces of sculpture and even larger murals. But the one gigantic bas-relief by Siegfried Charoux in the Sea and Ships Pavilion designed by Basil Spence had, in fact, less impact than the more modest Epstein. This may be because the latter was the more important work, as it was for me until my young son (as he then was) looked at the figure tip-toe poised with hands outstretched and asked "Where is the bicycle?". I could never again contemplate Epstein's

"Youth Advances" with unassociative aesthetic pleasure.

'The moral of this art/architectural activity was, I now feel sure, that art only has impact on large sections of the community when its subject is deeply emotive and when it is at the same time of such aesthetic consequence that no-one can contemplate it without empathic involvement. I fear that few of the works of our artist colleagues simultaneously met both criteria. But for those of us who knew every nook and cranny of the South Bank, the works of art were a recurring joy, a compensation for mental anguish and physical exhaustion.

'The work of the landscape architects, Marie Shepherd, H. F. Clark, Peter Shepheard and G. P. Youngman, was also accepted as though there was no surprise in 500 trees springing to immediate leaf-laden life in what, only a few months previously, had been a building contractor's desert. The tens of thousands of tulips (changed overnight into summer flowers), the turf, rocks, streams and waterfalls were all accepted as normality while I remained amazed that nature could be harnessed by our command into instantaneous activity.

ARCHITECTURE VERSUS DESIGN

'Associating the artists with the architects presented no problems. Each accepted the authority, wisdom and skills of the other; the task of the co-ordinating architects was the simple one of bringing together those of like mind and intention. Co-ordination of building with interior exhibition design was more difficult.

'Complete harmony existed only when the designer was responsible both for structure and content. This was so in the Lion and the Unicorn pavilion, designed by Robert Gooden and R. D. Russell and the Homes and Gardens building designed by Bronek Katz and Reginald Vaughan. Both groups of architects produced unassertive structures, concentrating their energies and interest on the contents. The Homes and Gardens pavilion was professionally competent and economic, the Lion and Unicorn a delicious romp which succeeded in demonstrating with humour and slightly wry tolerance what the official catalogue described as "two of the main qualities of the national character: realism and strength on the one hand and, on the other, independence and imagination".

'Those were heroic days! But where the interior designers and architects were different teams and equally self-opinionated, the co-ordinating architects and designers spent time which they could ill afford and patience which was in short supply to achieve at least a semblance of co-operation.

'The cause of this strain was an initial misconception of what the exhibition as a whole could achieve. All of us who were responsible for the initial concept of the South Bank exhibition fell cheerfully and willingly into the same trap. The exhibition should, we planned, tell the whole story of British history and achievement. Everything that could be said would be said: there would be brown owls and flatfish, a locomotive and aircraft, Anglo Saxons and Romans, chemistry, biology, physics and nuclear science, telescopes, agriculture and Darwin, all the Nobel Prize winners and Polar dogs, public health and the White Knight. All of British past and present was to be crammed into the twenty-nine acres of the South Bank site. It was to be a *narrative* exhibition on the assumption that visitors would take the scheduled route and absorb much, if not all, of what was displayed and captioned. The script was edited by Lionel

Birch and Laurie Lee, tens of thousands of descriptive words were carefully, and sometimes brilliantly, written and edited. Only a fraction of this verbosity was read. The theme convenors, who were responsible for the content of the exhibition, were determined that everything should be shown and explained; the interior exhibition designers tried to cram their gallon of exhibits into the pint pot of the buildings; the architects screamed wth righteous indignation as the mass of exhibits and display devices threatened to destroy the spatial quality of their buildings.

'There were exceptions: the exhibits designed by James Gardner enhanced Cadbury Brown's elegant "People of Britain" building, but more often structure and exhibits were at odds.

'The problem was most acute in the Dome of Discovery. The ten theme convenors were determined that nothing should be omitted which did credit to Britain; the team of exhibition designers filled the Dome solid; the architect protested but packing-it-in continued. Eventually so much was displayed as to make comprehension impossible and only a general memory of creditable British exploration, invention and industrial capacity remained in the mind of even the most devoted caption reader and exhibit viewer. The magnificent awe-inspiring interior space, designed with great sensitivity by Ralph Tubbs, was diminished to no useful purpose by the interior display. I should know, as the interior was one of my special responsibilities.

'The catalogue proclaimed that "the exhibition tells a continuous story" but it is doubtful whether more than a single sentence lingered in the mind of even those visitors who returned many times. The magic of the exhibition was that of place, of a mirage seen from the north bank which became a reality once

Signs for the South Bank Exhibition, Festival of Britain, 1951, by Milner Gray.

the turnstile had clicked. It was the total experience which was remembered and cherished: the Dome lying on the ground as though it had newly arrived from Mars, entering into its crypt and then up to be encompassed by a metallic sky; the Skylon poised for take-off; the fountains designed by H. T. Cadbury Brown which rose and fell over flaring gas; Richard Huws' great gusher of a water sculpture which cascaded a thousand gallons of water – when it was not choked by orange peel; the interior of the Shot Tower vanishing upwards into mystery; the night view across the river to the illuminated fairy palace Whitehall Court with its pinnacles embellished by a host of flags; light bedded into the Fairway to become glow-worms for dancing over. Amidst such marvels the wording of a caption, the meticulous positioning of a Design Council selected tea service took second place.

'The narrative served its essential purpose, however, in providing an armature for planning and a route for meticulous map readers. The mass of exhibits satisfied those who felt that this gave them their money's worth, but the exhibition would have been better than it was if the number of exhibits had been decimated, if a few could have symbolised the multitude, if the interiors of the buildings had been less cluttered with intellectual bric-a-brac.

'The Dome of Discovery was at its most dramatic when empty, when, on a bitterly

The Dome of Discovery, Festival of Britain, 1951. Architect: Ralph Tubbs OBE FRIBA.

cold evening in the winter of 1950, all the workmen on the site were invited to a celebratory meal, the roofs having been finally battened down on all the buildings. A few naked bulbs gave illumination, the dark areas were greater than the lit, braziers glowed with minimal warmth. The speeches of exhortation to greater effort and fewer trade union disputes were dreary and misconceived. The atmosphere became as frigid as the night when suddenly one man sent his paper plate (food eaten) whizzing across the void. In a moment a thousand plates were spinning, until the whole volume of the Dome was alive with white discs, as though invaded by flying fish. This was a magical moment which all the skills of the exhibition designers could not emulate.

'The interior of the Shot Tower was reduced in stature by the exhibition display, the Transport building not improved by the detailed story of the history of transportation in Britain which remained incomplete to the closing day – not that anyone except the theme convenors or the designers were conscious of this, or minded that some showcases were strangely empty. It is axiomatic that an exhibition must contain exhibits; many of them on the South Bank were splendid, many of the display devices ingenious, designed with exemplary professional skill and sometimes beautiful – but much of the effort which was harnessed to the narrative chariot was misconceived. I remember only the big things: the 74 inch reflecting telescope in the Dome, the steam locomotive, sailing boats, the cows (regularly milked), the husky dogs mushing on salt simulating snow. But this may well be a personal failing – a preference for image over idea – as all I remember of Wembley in 1924 is the Prince of Wales in butter, unsure whether the sculptor's refrigerated material came from Australia or New Zealand.

THE ENORMOUS BISCUIT

'For the co-ordinating architects and designers the two years preceding the opening days were continuous anguish and anxiety. There was peace only during the weekly evening meeting of the Design Group when the sense of common purpose and mutual understanding made the length of our agenda tolerable. It was a battle against time, against the weather which turned the South Bank into a frozen girder-strewn lunar lanscape, against labour diputes, against budget cuts, against bitter newspaper criticism, against the pundits (Profesor A. E. Richardson in particular) who predicted disaster when the number of expected visitors would inevitably cause panic and disaster, of prophecies that London's traffic would grind to a halt. I had a recurring dream in which the Design Group had been transmogrified into mice nibbling away at a ballroom-sized biscuit: the biscuit was the project and somehow or other we had to consume it before 4 May, 1951. But we did, more or less, manage to eat the cookie.

'On the night before the opening day I had been without sleep for 36 hours. At 4 am we decided it was time to remove the contractors' huts which were then still in the main gangway of the Dome of Discovery. As the walls came down and the floor panels were lifted rats scattered in all directions to be chased by joiners and painters, their physical exhaustion extinguished by the excitement of the hunt. By morning the rats were dead, the gangway swept and the carpet laid to receive the Royal Family.

'On the opening day it poured with rain, but inside the pavilions all, on the surface, was serene. The Royal Family rode the escalators in the Dome in solemn procession. The air was aflutter with congratulations. The Beaverbrook Press switched from condemnation to adulation. I managed to keep awake during a thanksgiving lunch in the Regatta restaurant and sleep-walked over the Bailey bridge to bed.

'The Festival, for that summer, was Britain. The close-knit Design Panel divided to nurse their special babies. I spent most

Downstream Area, South Bank Exhibition, 1951, at night. Co-ordinating architect: Sir Hugh Casson RDI.

DAVID POTTS

early mornings on the South Bank trying to get put right those things which had gone wrong and instructing contractors as they completed or corrected displays to the satisfaction of the theme convenors and my own conscience. It was an unnecessary but obligatory penance. When the gates opened our work stopped and I ate a coconut kiss with my coffee alone in the Turntable Cafe. The early mornings seem always to have been fine, the Fairway still unpopulated, the river sparkling as an attendant released a gargantuan net of balloons. For fifteen minutes the South Bank Fairway could have been the Piazza San Marco at dawn.

'Soon the boats were steaming to Battersea Pleasure Gardens. Here I had no responsibility, as Gerald Barry had decided, to our chagrin, that the self-righteous young men of the South Bank were ill-suited to the design of a fun fair. He may have been right – he certainly was in appreciating that we physically could not have coped. James Gardner turned mud into popular pleasure, and the Baroque/Regency/Gothic stage setting of Battersea was certainly successful, although its contribution to architecture and design was minimal.

'In the meanwhile Basil Spence had completed the Exhibition of Industrial Power in Glasgow, Brian Peake displayed science and technology at the Science Museum, James Holland was afloat in the Exhibition Ship "Campania" and Willy de Mayo watched his crops and cattle at the Farm and Factory Exhibition in Ulster. Hugh Casson hovered over the South Bank and the architectural conclave in Poplar and nobly represented us all as he escorted a seemingly endless procession of very important people around the transitory city which we together had created. Art festivals, regional festivals and village festivals proliferated; some activity to celebrate Festival Year was initiated in 2000 cities, towns and villages.

'In London, Jack Howe completed what was left of the programme for street decoration after his budget had been slashed – but his magnificent four-pointed star remained to dominate Northumberland Avenue.

'The official catalogue lists 48 architects, 102 designers, 31 theme convenors and three tightly set pages of consultants and advisers. The talent of Britain had been allowed to bloom in unison for five months – the result surprised even those who had been responsible for the concept.

'On 30 September the massed bands of the Brigade of Guards beat the Retreat, the dancers on the Fairway linked arms and sang Auld Lang Syne, and euphoria was diminished only when the cleaners arrived to sweep up the daily rubbish mountain.

'On the next day I walked round the exhibition for the last time. It had already assumed the air of a ghost town. Exhibits were being removed, the valuable objects were being packed, and the demolition gangs were mustering. A public sale was held on the site and South Bank aficionados struggled to the Underground clutching plaster doves, Race chairs, light fittings and butterflies immortalized in plastic cubes. The Treasury had spent too long quibbling about a fair price for the Dome and the Skylon and the earlier enthusiasm of potential buyers had evaporated, so they also were demolished and sold for scrap. Soon the Festival Hall was marooned in a sea of exhibition debris. The carnival was over.'

International Recognition 1952–1964

The Festival of Britain established Misha Black as one of the foremost exhibition designers in the country. But his work in co-ordinating the up-stream section of the South Bank Exhibition was only an example of his skill as a business man, and he found full scope for his abilities in this field in his work for Design Research Unit until, in 1959, he also began to teach as a Professor of the Royal College of Art.

In 1952 he designed coronation decorations for Queen Elizabeth II and wrote a number of articles including 'The Crown Furnishes' and 'Coronations Celebrated'. This was the year in which his first marriage was dissolved, although he still continued to see his children and have an influence on their lives.

In 1953 he designed a reception room in the new Time-Life Building in Bond Street; a new millinery department for Peter Robinson Ltd; the 'Mersey Room' restaurant in Liverpool for Lewis's Ltd; a central maintenance base for BOAC at London Airport; a showroom for Keyser Bonder in London; and the 'Conquest of the Desert' exhibition in Jerusalem.

In 1954 his work included designing a new show-room for the London Electricity Board in Regent Street; the Drapers' Chamber of Trade, Harley Street; the British exhibit at the Tenth Triennale, Milan; moulded plastic handles for Godfrey Holmes Ltd; judging an illuminated sign competition; and writing articles on 'The Designer at Work' and 'The Architect and the Interior'.

Clifford Hatt's drawing of Misha Black's design for the decoration of the streets of Westminster for the Coronation, 1952. Sir Hugh Casson was architect in charge of the decorations.

STEWART BALE/DRU

'The Mersey Room' Restaurant, Lewis's Ltd, Liverpool. Designers: Misha Black, Robert Gutmann FSIA, and Gunther Hoffstead of Design Research Unit. 1954.

(Right) Tray for small components for use on benches at the BOAC Headquarters, London Airport. Designers: Misha Black and Kenneth Bayes, FRIBA MSIA. 1951–55.

(Below) The Engineering Hall, BOAC Headquarters at London Airport showing the hydraulics and electrical workshops in the foreground. The architects for the building were Sir Owen Williams and Partners. The layout of the workshops was carried out by a BOAC committee of technicians which included Misha Black and Kenneth Bayes FRIBA MSIA, of Design Research Unit, 1951–55.

Instrument and radio shop work bench, BOAC Headquarters at London Airport, designed 1951–55. Designers: Misha Black and Kenneth Bayes FRIBA MSIA.

DRU

The hall and main staircase of the Time-Life building, New Bond Street, London W1 designed by Sir Hugh Casson and Misha Black. The architect for the building was Michael Rosenauer FRIBA AIA. The walls were Derbydene Fossil marble, and floor and stairs travertine and unpolished Derbydene. The staircase balustrade is of brass-enriched black leather, designed by R. Y. Goodden. On the marble shelf below the stairs stands a maquette of the sculpture screen by Henry Moore which stood at the second floor level on the Bond Street elevation. The curtain is 'Chiave' design by Tibor Reich. 1952.

DRU

DRU

SWINDON PRESS/DRU

(Above) Exterior view of entrance of London Electricity Board showrooms in Regent Street. Designers Misha Black, Alexander Gibson FRIBA AADipl, and H. Diamond BArch ARIBA, all of Design Research Unit. The curved showcase and entrance doors on the right are part of the original front designed by Maxwell Fry. c 1954.

(Left) 'Conquest of the Desert' Exhibition, Jerusalem, September 1953. This was designed and produced for (UNESCO), (WHO) and the (ILO). Architect: John Diamond, BArch ARIBA. Display: Austin Frazer, MSIA. Consultant: Misha Black OBE FSIA, all of Design Research Unit.

DRU

(Above The conference room, Drapers' Chamber
of Trade, 4 Harley Street, London W1. Designer:
Misha Black. The table is extendable and the shades
to the light fitting are of red leather. 1954.

(Right) The entrance hall of the Drapers' Chamber
of Trade, 4 Harley Street, London W1, designed by
Misha Black. The banquette was designed by Misha
Black in collaboration with Ernerst Race Ltd. 1954.

In 1954 Misha Black was made President of the Society of Industrial Artists and Designers. Work for and talks to the society had been a major spare-time occupation for Misha Black before, during and after the war. He was a Council member from 1938 to 1952 and from 1956 to 1957. By the outbreak of war the SIA had gained 300 members. Its real development, however, began in 1945 when it disbanded all its members and set up an examining board to vet applications for re-admittance – with the result that some original members failed to get back.

Today there are about 6700 fellows, members, licentiates and associates, covering all aspects of industrial design, but still mainly concerned with graphics. The society has also widened its interest to include a sprinkling of engineers. In 1963 it changed its name to give recognition to the wider scope.

In 1954 DRU opened a Dublin office and Thurloe Conolly joined the Design Research Unit of Ireland as designer-in-charge. That year DRU organised the first exhibition in Dublin of international industrial design for the Irish Arts Council. It followed two years later with an exhibition of all-Irish industrial design which toured four other Irish cities.

Meanwhile, in 1955, Misha Black worked on such projects as an exhibition of Anglo-Jewish Art and History at the Victoria & Albert Museum;

(Above) Moulded plastic door handle for Godfrey Holmes Ltd designed by Misha Black, 1949.

(Right) Moulded plastic door handle for Godfrey Holmes Ltd designed by Misha Black. This was a cheap handle for the Government's working-class housing programmes. The shaped knob ensured an easier turn than conventional handles, 1949.

JOHN MALTBY/DRU

Exhibition of Anglo-Jewish art and history designed for The Council for the Tercentenary of the Resettlement of the Jews in the British Isles by Misha Black and Ronald Ingles FSIA, of Design Research Unit. The exhibition was held at the Victoria and Albert Museum in January, 1956.

MILLAR & HARRIS/DRU

(Above) China and glass department for the Army and Navy Stores designed by Misha Black with assistants Ellis Miles ARIBA and Philip Lucye ARIBA, 1954.

(Right) Lighting fitting for Hume Atkins and Co Ltd, Letchworth, Herts. These fittings were intended for schools, canteens and commercial and industrial buildings, 1953.

PHILLIP TURNER/DRU

MILLAR & HARRIS/DRU

(Left) Stand at the British Industries Fair, 1955, for British Celanese Ltd. Designers: Misha Black and Alexander Gibson FRIBA AADipl, both of Design Research Unit. The photograph shows the central platform leading to the tower of plastic balls suspended over a bubbling pool.

(Below) The British exhibit at the Tenth Triennale, Milan, in 1954, designed by Misha Black and displaying Race furniture.

DRU

Joan and Misha Black on their wedding day, 15 July 1955.

light fittings for Hume, Atkins and Company; Army & Navy Stores shop-fitting and a stand for British Celanese at the British Industries Fair. His articles, this year, included 'The Role of Designers in Industry' and 'A Quarter Century of Design.'

He also met and married Edna Joan Fairbrother, daughter of George Septimus Fairbrother, an engineer. Joan, who had studied modern languages at Oxford, was working for UNESCO when she first met Misha. They were together in Mexico where Misha was devising the first exhibition of UNESCO's work, following the first international conference of UNESCO, held in 1947. Misha and Joan found each other's company so entertaining that a friendship developed that resulted in a very happy marriage. Extrovert, social, knowledgeable, Joan could support Misha in the wide-ranging demands of his life, travelling with him and attending conferences with him although she also ran the home and put her education to use in social work, teaching backward children in a school in Battersea.

In 1956 Misha was commissioned to design the interior of the P & O – Orient Lines ship, the SS Oriana.

He wrote about this:

'There is one fundamental rule for all interior design, whether on land or sea: the atmosphere it is desired to create must be clearly envisaged before the first line is drawn. Basic planning must take precedence over all other considerations, but even at the planning stage the designer must have at least a general picture in the mind's eye of the effect which he and his clients are aiming to produce. This is the crux of the interior design problem. If the atmosphere is not right, then the careful detailing, the expert attention to furniture and fabrics, and the skilled balancing of lighting effects will be nullified ...

'Design today varies to a greater degree than in any previous period. It can be sleek and expensive and luxurious as a custom-built Rolls Royce; it can be as exciting and brash as an American limousine: it can be as restrained and elegant as an Italian car body by Pinin Farina; as sturdy as a small British family saloon or as emotive of speed as a racing car. Where amongst these many images of contemporary design does the ship-owner find the style suitable to his needs? The answer may be found by analysing the requirements that are the base from which the design of any passenger ship must grow:

1 The planning of the public rooms, entrances and staircase must allow for

The P & O Orient Lines' ship 'Oriana'. Design Research Unit's contribution to the ship included the first class lounge, a children's playroom and a special version of the ship's badge on the bows. 1959.

easy passenger circulation within the ship for the rooms themselves to function efficiently.

2 The atmosphere of well-being must be established from the first step of the gangway to the end of the voyage. The scheme of decoration must thus seem appropriate and comfortable during heavy weather in the Bay of Biscay and equally satisfactory with a following wind in the Red Sea.

3 The public rooms must seem light and airy with a tang of the sea during the daytime and yet enclosed and self-contained when the curtains are drawn at night.

4 The atmosphere of a great ship must be retained for those who enjoy the sea, without its impinging too drastically on the less fortunate for whom a voyage is synonymous with sea-sickness tablets.

5 The design of the different public areas must reflect and encourage their intended usage.

6 In a large ship there must be sufficient variation in the design of its different areas to combat visual boredom.

7 Easy access must be provided to all services without allowing the duct runs and removable sections to be obtrusive.

8 The whole scheme of decoration must be sufficiently positive to give a definite personality to the ship equal to the individuality of its external form. The passenger should end his journey with positive pleasurable memories of the special world in which he has lived for days or weeks and as glad to travel on that ship again as he is delighted to return to an excellent hotel which he knows well.'

JOHN MALTBY/DRU

A general view of the tourist library, 'Oriana', P & O Orient Lines. Co-ordinating architects for the public rooms: Design Research Unit. Partners in charge: Misha Black, Milner Gray RDI PPSIA and Kenneth Bayes FRIBA FSIA. 1959.

(Upper) D.1000 diesel hydraulic locomotive 2700 hp for British Railways Western Region. Designers Misha Black and J. Beresford-Evans FSIA. 1956–62.

(Lower) 2000 hp electric locomotive for British Railways (Southern region). Bodywork designers: Misha Black and J. Beresford-Evans FSIA, of Design Research Unit working in association with engineers of British Railways. 1956–62.

In partnership with Kenneth Bayes, Misha Black met all his own stated requirements. The Oriana was launched by Princess Alexandra on 3 November, 1959.

In the meanwhile, still in 1956, design work included the first two designs of locomotives for British Rail. This was the beginning of a relationship that was to lead to DRU being made responsible for the entire overall corporate identity programme for British Rail, including the design of new uniforms.

In 1957 another widening of interests was the inauguration of the International Council of Societies of Industrial Design which held its first General Assembly in Stockholm from 15 to 19 September. Misha Black was prominent in the development of the organisation and was Vice-President from 1957 to 59 and President from 1959 to 61. He acted as Chairman of the first ICSID/UNESCO seminar on Industrial Design Education in Bruges, Belgium, in 1964. He was also Chairman of the Second ICSID Seminar at Ulm, West Germany, in 1967 and of the third ICSID Seminar in Syracuse, USA, in 1967.

In his handling of such meetings Misha Black was outstanding. Nobody who has experienced an international conference with Black as chairman would have failed to appreciate the logic and coherence of his summing up at the end of each session. Speech would follow long speech; the audience would struggle to concentrate on the simultaneous translation; hell would seem to have been paved with good intentions – and then Misha would sum up. In a quarter of an hour the essence of every speaker's words would have been distilled, collated, put in context of further progress for us all, and the meeting dismissed to lunch or tea on a wave of euphoria and excited chatter. The effect was extraordinary. It was a supreme demonstration of his ability to project ideas. That he was a practising creative designer as well seemed an incredible bonus.

*(Above) Misha Black's design for the Kayser
Bondor showroom, 24 Albemarle Street, London
W1 in 1957. This was designed in association with
Sir Hugh Casson. The mirror wall has concealed
stock cupboards and the screen to the selling areas
is lacquered green and gold.*

*(Right) The millinery department of Peter
Robinson, Oxford Circus. Architects: Misha
Black, Alexander Gibson FRIBA AADipl, and
Norman Whicheloe ARIBA AADipl, all of
Design Research Unit.*

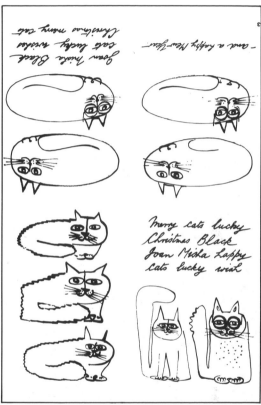

(Above left) Committee members at the International Congress of Societies of Industrial Design, Ulm, 1965.

(Above right) Christmas card designed by Misha Black.

HOCHSCHULE FÜR GESTALTUNG, ULM

Also in 1957 Misha Black became a Royal Designer for Industry. He was to be master of the faculty from 1974 to 1975. His son, Oliver, was born on the 8th of January. At this time Misha became exhibition architect for the Furniture Exhibition, not only designing stands but the main feature as well, and co-ordinating the general display. He held this position for three years.

In 1958 Misha Black designed the 'My Lady' range of saucepans for Ernest Stevens Ltd and a stewpan and stainless steel saucepan for Judge. The Judge saucepan won a Design Award in 1960.

In 1959 Misha Black was made Professor of Industrial Design (Engineering) at the Royal

College of Art. Much of his most important writing, from this time on, set out to define the right training for industrial designers. 1959 was also the year of the Magdalen Street Project, the initiative for which came from the Civic Trust. Misha Black was employed as co-ordinating architect and wrote about it:

'The Magdalen Street Project has been well described as a face-lift, and cosmetics are no cure for radical disease. But many of our streets are basically sound and agreeable: their character has been spoiled by a few shoddy buildings prominently sited, by the insensitive conversion of houses into shops, by ill-treated trees, by poorly designed street furniture which has unnecessarily multiplied, by over-head wires criss-crossing the street. This was the state of Magdalen Street.'

Special feature at the Furniture Exhibition, 1957, designed by Misha Black with assistant architect John Bruckland and graphic designer Robert Perritt.

JOHN MALTBY/DRU

JOHN MALTBY/DRU

JOHN MALTBY/DRU

(Above) 'My Lady' Judge vitreous enamel saucepan for Ernest Stevens Ltd. Misha Black and Ronald Armstrong of Design Research Unit. 1958.

(Left) Judge stainless steel saucepan set for Ernest Stevens Ltd designed by Misha Black and Ronald Armstrong of Design Research Unit, 1958.

DRU

(Opposite page) Three views of Magdalen Street, Norwich, after the improvement scheme was carried out for the Civic Trust in 1959–60. Co-ordinating architect: Misha Black.

(Above) The rehabilitation of Corby Village for Corby Development Corporation and the provision of new housing. Design Research Unit.

Working with the enthusiastic co-operation of the Norwich City Council and the City Engineer, they redesigned the street lighting and street furniture of Magdalen Street and helped the individual owners of the properties with colour schemes and lettering. The result was lively, visually interesting, a good advertisement for the business people and a hope for towns of the future. People came from all over the country to see Magdalen Street and it sparked off comparable schemes in Burslem, Windsor and Croydon and the interest of many other towns.

Corby Old Village was another area 'face-lifted' in this scheme. This was in 1961 when Misha Black's work included the twin engine Beagle 206 and the small mammal house at the London Zoo, opened in May, 1967. Kenneth Bayes, Misha Black's partner in this project, has said that his study of the problem of creating a satisfactory environment for mentally subnormal people helped in designing the mammal house in that both were for 'clients' unable to express their needs and whose experiences an architect was unable to share. For the mammal house project, research had to be carried out to find the best possible environment for each animal and, especially, to ensure there would be no adverse effects on their health or breeding habits from such factors as the reversal of night and day, which was achieved in a special section for nocturnal animals, called 'The Moonlight World'.

1961 also saw Misha Black designing the 'Newcastle Looks Ahead' exhibition in the Laing Art Gallery, visited by more than 11 000 people in the first few days.

The Journal for 26 April, 1961 described Misha Black as *'A man with a plan to set Tyne alight.'*

1962 saw the first of Misha Black's post office schemes, in Knightsbridge. He also designed the silver coffee set which was Eric Marshall's chosen prize for the Duke of Edinburgh Award for Elegant Design in 1961.

News of this coffee set even reached Borneo, where the *North Borneo News,* Sandakan (No 29, May 1962) reported, in a photo caption: *'Prince Philip admires an elegant and modernistic silver coffee pot prior to presenting it to Mr Eric Marshall at the Design Centre in London's Haymarket.'*

Misha, a recognised authority on public interiors by this time (he had written a book for Batsford in 1960) was appointed as interior design consultant to the Co-operative Insurance Society; but his growing interest was in the design of locomotives.

In September, 1962, he took a continental train journey and made a day-to-day diary of it which illustrates the attention to detail which went into his designs for British Rail.

'The Continental entrance to Victoria station, is clean, agreeable, nondescript. Porter old and friendly. A good beginning. Station concourse sordid and litter-strewn. Platform peaceful. Locomotive E 5015. Clean and efficient looking. Golden Arrow symbols on side

DRU

HENK SNOEK/DRU

DRU

(Opposite below) The Charles Clore Pavilion for
Small Mammals at the London Zoo, Regents Park.
Entrance to the pavilion from the Regents Canal
Bank. Architects: Black, Bayes and Gibson.
General Contractors: G. E. Wallis & Sons Ltd.

(Opposite above) The Charles Clore Pavilion for
Small Mammals at the London Zoo, Regents Park,
1967.

(Above) Branch post office, 55 Knightsbridge. An
example of an experimental series of modernised
branch post offices in London designed by Misha
Black and Design Research Unit in association with
Sir Hugh Casson, 1962.

(Right) Coffee set in silver and lignum vitæ designed
by Misha Black with Kenneth Lamble FSI as his
associate. This was chosen by Eric Marshall as his
prize for elegant design presented by The Duke of
Edinburgh. T. J. Boucher of the Royal College of
Art made the coffee set. 1961.

JOHN MALTBY/DRU

a good idea but coarsely designed and not well placed. Effect of train as a whole marred by old luggage truck between locomotive and first coach.

'First inspection spoilt by the locomotive at platform entry end. Very dirty. Side windows thick with grime of many days. Train mainly Pullman coaches built 1951. Exterior colour agreeable. Few standard SR green coaches so different as to be acceptable, but no impact of a special train. Pullman interior a riot of un-related patterns. Heavy and claustrophobic. These "old" Pullman coaches dramatically demonstrate how good the new ones are.

'Crockery pleasantly patterned. But as cups always up-ended on table the first sight a typographically illiterate advertisement for their manufacturer. Service and sandwiches good, coffee acceptable but with a tang of Nescafé.

'Trianon Bar advertised on menu but non-existent. Dover station clean, efficient, institutional. SS Invicta. Black and white with buff funnel. Rust streaked, looks its age, not inviting on a dull rain-misted day. Ship interior redolent of the 1930s. Dull, shoddily detailed.

'The whole British side of the journey very efficient but completely lacking glamour. Only positively good mark the service of antique porters and stewards and the younger Pullman and ship crew.

'The one bright spot the cover of the infor-mation booklet in the cabin! That reminded us that we are not Edwardian travellers.'

In Calais he wrote:

'A minimal shed for the Calais station. The Flèche d'Or a collection of miscellaneous coaches.

1   Battered luggage van. Dark green obscured by dirt to a brown/black patina.

2   Pullman coaches, cream upper part, indigo blue below waist. Broad lining in yellow. Lettering crude and unskilled in execution.
3   1st and 2nd class coaches patinated to the beaten brown/black finish.
4   New electric locomotive medium grey/green with cast aluminium trim.
5   At Amiens two new stainless steel coaches and a blue/cream Wagon-Lit were added.

'The train visually un-coordinated. Where coaches were of the same period and colour even, they sometimes varied in gauge and window detail. 1st class Pullman interior shabby. As Edwardian as the British side, but down-at-heel. Wider gauge gives sense of space. Good marks for white table linen and clean linen antimacassars covering whole seat head and looking like nuns' head-dresses. Stewards smart in clean white linen jackets. Crockery and cutlery commonplace. Knives as heavy as hammers.

D.1000 diesel hydraulic locomotive, 2700 hp, with crest for British Railways Western Region.

SAM LAMBERT/DRU

2000 hp diesel hydraulic locomotive built by the North British Locomotive Co Ltd for British Transport Commission, D.600 class. Design consultant Misha Black.

'Lunch adequate but poor value at £1.15.0. With a half bottle of wine, a whisky and coffee – £2.5.0 per head. One expects better for that. Arrived Paris exactly on time. A muddle off-loading luggage at Gare du Nord, but after that plenty of porters.

'The general impression was of an unkempt journey. There was no sense of a special train with the glamour and service one expects. I had some sympathy with the hysterical English woman who, after refusing most of the lunch for one not particularly good reason after another said "I *thought* this was 'The Golden Arrow'". Everything suggested that BR and SNF were not trying any more as far as The Golden Arrow is concerned.

12 September. Gare de Lyon

'An opportunity to see a wide range of French trains.

1 *"Standard" coaches.* Dark green (similar to BR locomotive green) when newly painted. Roof black. All allowed to patinate to negative black/brown. Lettering orange-ochre.

2 *Steam locomotives* (of which very few were seen) dirty dark green or black encrusted with pipe-work and rust. Powerful, impressive primeval relics.

3 *Diesel cars.* Cream above waist, crimson below. Cream drops to form "V" at nose. Cream carried over roof. Detailing

adequate but unrefined. Standard local trains and a few diesel cars carry yellow advertisements at each side of coach entrance doors. Not a good idea.

4   Suburban electric corrugated unpainted aluminium or stainless steel.
5   TEE trains much in evidence.
6   A few stainless steel coaches.
7   Miscellaneous Wagon-Lit coaches in traditional dark indigo blue with impressive cast bronze heraldic badges. (A brand new traditional coach, British built, handsome with strong yellow lining on dark blue. Spoilt by poor detail and lettering sprayed on with ragged "halo".)
8   An odd local diesel railcar in "desert sand".
9   Mail-vans maroon.
10 The new electric locomotives mid grey/green with polished cast aluminium trim.

He concluded:

'The general impression after three long journeys on French railways was that there was no recognisable or memorable livery. To a romantic British eye, the dark indigo blue Wagon-Lits were nostalgic of Blue Trains, Trans-Siberian Expresses and adventure, but they were in fact only rarely seen. The present was clearly typified by the TEE and the new stainless steel coaches, both of which are described below. The image of the Wagon-Lit coach is now vitiated by the occasional appearance of a Wagon-Lit of unpainted stainless steel.

'Some visual confusion is caused by the shape and colour of the new French railcars. These are painted "post-office" red up to the waist and cream above; class numbers orange. At first glance they look like the TEE, thus reduce the TEE impact and are, in themselves, not specially distinguished. The unifying factor is the new grey/green electric locomotives which are now sufficiently numerous to draw attention from the miscellaneous array of other liveries.'

Misha Black also travelled on, and made notes about, the Mistral, the TEE Ligure (Breda: Milan 1957); the TEE Cisalpin (which took him from Milan to Paris); the Italian railways; the Swiss train which took him from Lausanne to Zurich; the TEE ticino; and Il Settebello; finally commenting:

'There was no impact of a coherent livery policy in any of three railway systems on which I travelled. The most positive element was the crimson/cream of the TEE trains. For the rest I am left with a series of un-coordinated images and have only been able to separate out my memory of one system from another by reference to my notes.'

All he learned from this time of observation was made an object lesson for the design of the diesel hydraulic locomotives he worked on with J. Beresford-Evans and the engineers of the British Railways workshops. It was also relevant to his work on a corporate identity scheme for British Rail devised from 1965 to 1969 but was later superseded.

(Opposite above and below left) 25 kV 3200 hp ac/electric locomotive for British Railways. Designers Misha Black and J. Beresford-Evans FSIA. 1956–62

(Opposite below right); 2200 hp diesel-hydraulic locomotive for British Railways, Western Region, 1959. The Bristolian at Ealing Broadway. Consultant Designers: Misha Black, J. Beresford-Evans FSIA, both of Design Research Unit in collaboration with engineers of British Railways Workshops, Swindon.

SAM LAMBERT/DRU

SAM LAMBERT/DRU

BRITISH RAILWAYS/DFRU

Work in 1963 included the Chairman's Room and Boardroom, Millbank Tower, for the English Steel Corporation.

Misha Black also went to Rio de Janeiro to lecture and, once more, kept a diary, later published as *A South American Diary.*

8 April

'Touch down in torrential rain, at 5.30 am already oppressively humid. First sight of South America, "CINZANO" in 20 ft high letters on the hills cupping the airfield. The airport building large, bleak and anonymous – apart from 60 ft murals. These agreeable decorations take the eye from shoddy workmanship, towel-less lavatories and the "Arte Regional" which echo Birmingham instead of Brazil.

Galeao Airport

'Over Rio de Janeiro, white buildings stacked against the sea. From above the buildings an army of white cubes whose stolid march to the sea's edge has been stopped only by the inviolate sand. A magnificent harbour of linked lagoons.

Buenos Aires: Ezeiza Airport

'Ponderous new buildings. A good read for the hour's drive into the city. First impression

The Chairman's Room for English Steel, Millbank Tower, London, SW1. 1963.

DRU

Board Room for Vickers Ltd on the 30th Floor, Vickers House, Millbank Tower, London SW1. The walls and columns are panelled with solid walnut boarding, laid vertically in random widths and detailed to follow the curve of the building. Designers: Misha Black and Bryan Rodda DipArch ARIBA, of Design Research Unit. Table designed by Frank Height DesRCA AMIMechE MSIA. Architects for the building: Ronald Ward & Partners. 1963.

of Buenos Aires, big, untidy, Edwardian. Micro-Omnibus the local transport. Passenger packed, decorated like an English barge – complete with coloured lights at night; bumpers great cages of wrought iron chromium plated. Each bus different, each a pleasure.

'A totter through the streets and then to sleep off 22 airborne hours.

9 April

'A magnificent morning, bright with sun yet Autumn cool. First meeting at Institute Nacional de Tecnologia Industrial (INTI), the Argentinian DSIR. The Centro de Investigacion del Diseno Industrial (Industrial Design Research Centre) recently formed an off-shoot of INTI. Where CoID was in 1945 but with advantage of accumulated European experience. Press conference at the British Embassy. Reporters friendly and cynical but papers and television kindly and well-disposed. Time off to see the town. Architecture non-descript. French and British Victorian monumental. A new city without architectural distinction. Wide streets establish its character. Could be a slightly down-at-heel Madrid; Florida early shop-lined pedestrian precinct closed to traffic after 10 am. Six million population in BA, 10m with outer suburbs, pleasant but unkept. Holes in every pavement, much digging for new electric cables but no attempt to reinstate surface. Walk with half an eye cast down to avoid pot holes or mole mounds.

'Ridiculous how minor top dressing seals an impression. Buenos Aires pot holes no more important than Moscow's immaculately clean streets. Or is the trivial symptomatic of the fundamental?

'The first lecture; audience of 60, teachers, architects, designers, students. The usual Marx Brothers start with impotent slide projections and a film escaped from its reel to lie a tangled mess. A human chain formed to disentangle it. Late start but everything made to work. Seemed a success. The Royal College film greatly admired. The professors of architecture envious. Some 13 of them run a school in BA with 5000 students. Mostly part-time, studying in three shifts.

'Consecutive translation works well. Slows the tempo but provides time to think.

11 April

'Day off for Easter holiday. Strange for Easter to herald the Autumn. More sightseeing. The whole of BA now covered. First impressions not amended. People intelligent, handsome, friendly. Oddly English looking, very few "typical" Latin-American. Women attractive. Seem well-disposed to Britain. English names everywhere. Harrods in the Florida. Down to the river Plate. A great expanse of dun water; opposite shore not visible. Café au lait horizon against blue sky. Dinner with the director of the Anglophile society. Steak clearly from a celestial animal unknown in Britain.

12 April

'The suburbs. Thousands of acres, a hundred miles of tree-lined streets. In the working-class districts undulating granite sets for the roads. Some colonial houses, single storied, pink washed walls. House follows house of prefabricated cast-iron frame units with corrugated iron for walls and roofs; colour washed. Exported industrialised buildings from Britain of the late 19th century. Squatters' villages, huts from motor-car packing cases; television aerials on shacks. Still summer hot, lunch with architects, barbecue on the roof, London talk.

13 April

'Town improves with knowing. Good buildings appear – slim new apartment blocks. Concrete frames (before cladding) as frail as a bird's bones. Many parks, children's playgrounds, several stadia each to hold 100 000 for football. Crowds at the Cathedral, sermon broadcast outside. Police armed, soldiers in trucks at corners.

'At night La Boca. Italian Argentinian Soho infinitely multiplied, noise to drown a revolution. "My bonny lies over the Ocean" and "Tipperary" in our honour. Samba lines between the table. Before that, South American dancing at a theatre, its interior just redecorated; red as a fresh wound.

14 April

'A day at the races. The Jockey Club at San Isidro. Ground beautifully kept, elegant stands for all classes. Each stand holds some 15 000 massed heads shouting themselves off. I am clearly not a racing type. In the evening our kindly guides from INTI determined that we shall see another typical restaurant. So to Al Asador. In the window a circular spit 10 ft in diameter. At its centre a log fire which could roast an ox, hors d'oeuvres of hot sausages, black pudding or a cornish pasty. Then a great chunk of meat or half a chicken off Vulcan's spit, a salad and a crème caramel.

15 April

'The first seminar; the table a tangled mess of wire and earphones for simultaneous translation. Two tape machines, and a slide projector complicate the scene. Twenty architects, designers, engineers and aficionados thread their way to their places. Earphones on – we start.

'I speak for three hours; intervals for coffee and questions but almost non-stop. The seminar clearly to be an endurance test. Twelve times three hours equals 36 – have I enough to say? Evident, not a talk to beginners. Many have read all the books, are packed with theory, interested in turning theory into practice. We get down to a definition of Industrial Design.

16 – 17 April

'The second seminar and public lecture in the evening. Today back to the seminar and to lunch with the British Engineering Association.

'Talk on Atomic Energy by Mr Evans Morgan, an Argentinian of Welsh descent from Patagonia. The Welsh colony now 100 years old. They speak Welsh and Spanish. The links with Britain still strong and emotional – but USA taking over. America will provide the long term credits which Britain cannot or will not. Argentinians shake their heads about inflation, unemployment, unstable governments, unfavourable balance of trade.

18 April

'The seminars continue. Surprising how much there is to say. A comment that I am not telling them anything new or original – but there is nothing new to be said; what are needed now are detailed techniques, the accumulation of experience, the establishment of organised education, the slow growth of a profession. Lunch at the British Embassy. An Edwardian house. Impressive, agreeable, sophisticated, nondescript. Furniture from an antique stage set. Tonight steel helmeted soldiers with tommy guns at the street corners. The political ice precariously thin.

19 April

'The seminar now a working group. Deep into discussions, of design methodology; objective and subjective design; conceptual and additive approach. Another "public" lecture. Pretty farcical. Small audience, slide projector breaks down, degenerates into argument with German professor of architecture.

'Argentinians remain gloomy. Nothing is possible until they find a way of establishing a stable government.

'Zebra crossings just installed. Loud speakered voices insist on pedestrian rights but still a battle of wits between walkers and drivers.

20 April

'A day off. by car to the Hurlingham Clubs deteriorate into a desert of single and two-storied houses, shops, empty lots. Miles of road to upkeep. In poor condition, car rides like a bronco. Only the hot sun makes this southern subtopia tolerable. Milk carts decorated with fair ground colour and patterns. Lorries brightly coloured, elaborately enriched. But men's ties sober blacks or greys. Doors to expensive apartment houses dark green with polished brass trim; 5ft wide.

21 April

'The Colon Theatre. A veritable Scala. Argentina Milanese. Elegant.

22 April

'The sixth seminar. Seminarists still with me. On to Anthropometrics, Ergonomics and Market Research.

23 April

'The seminars now a habit. Three hours each morning, all still attentive. I feel as though I have been talking for a lifetime – a marathon of words. Dinner in a house left from the 1890s. Trees remain to shield it from the surrounding towers of expensive apartment blocks. Experimental architecture in converted coach house, art nouveau furniture in the house, a Leger on the wall. Commanded to visit the Mayor of Buenos Aires. An architect. German/Argentinian looking like a Prussian officer. The Town Hall an Edwardian fantasy.

24 April

'A lecture at the Academy of Beaux Arts. A converted mansion of 400 students working in three shifts. Fine Arts in isolation, Principal anxious to introduce design. The RCA film applauded, the room packed with students. So used to consecutive translation that I fear I shall never again be able to talk at normal speed.

25 April

'Hot. Humidity 90 per cent. But no flagging at the ninth seminar. A visit to the SIAM works. Refrigerators, motor cars, fans, electric equipment. Would not shame Birmingham. Large scale industry but most products still made under licence. Beginning to adapt UK and USA models, new products coming up. Staff design office, intelligently and sensitively directed by young men supported by Chairman. Spot design discussion. Impressive. But factory working at half capacity –

the depression. Sheet steel imported from Japan. Back to the City over rutted roads, lorries lurch like anxious charging elephants.

26 April

'The last seminar. A design criticism meeting. Argentinian objects on table – all comment. I sum up. Exciting and successful – should have had more of this practical discussion. At ATMA works. Electric irons, switches, electrical gear. Impeccable, clean, organised, crèche for children, ready for expansion which awaits political and economic stability. To inspect a first full scale mock up of an all Argentinian sports car, to see fibreglass boat and to lecture at the Faculty of Architecture. Then dinner with the seminarists at the University Club. They stage a parody of my conducting a seminar. Brilliantly contrived, hilarious. I am pleased with the seminars. Shall be more expert another time – but they worked well. In Argentina there is an Industrial Design nexus, from this a professional organisation could grow if the present industrial depression can politically be halted. It was worth doing, a small token of international co-operation, a link in the historic chain of Anglo-Argentinian friendship. New week. Maldonado will lecture, then Tapiovaara starts a new seminar – they are determined to build their profession on a basis of accumulated knowledge.'

Misha Black then went on to Cordoba, Sao Paulo and Rio de Janeiro, flying home on 11 May.

'On BOAC Comet. Interior in polite good taste, well finished, efficient. All the British virtues.

'For me a welcome return to the climate I understand. But we could do with an injection of Brazilian optimism: the British body is strong enough to survive the treatment.'

HEINZ ZIMRAN/DRU

DRU

These three illustrations show rolling stock and stations for the Victoria line. The visual aspects of the line were supervised by a design panel including Misha Black, London Transport's design consultant. Some detailed design work was carried out by Design Research Unit in collaboration with the London Transport Architects, Chief Mechanical Engineer (Railways) and Chief Signals Engineer. 1968.

In 1964 Misha Black was asked to design trains and stations on the new Victoria underground line. The *Evening News* of 9 June reported:

'Bright Look for Vic Line Stations. The new Victoria Line underground stations are going to be brighter, quieter and easier on the eye.

'For a month, 52-year-old Professor Misha Black, London Transport design consultant, and a team of experts have been building three 60 ft mock-ups of suggested station designs on a disused platform at Aldwych station.

'On Tuesday, London Transport Executive Officials will probably make their choice.

'The mock-ups suggest that the stations will retain their tunnel shape, but a light grey plastic material may replace tiles for the walls.

'Easy-to-see illuminated information boxes, with maps and station names will be offset from the walls.

Lighting

'Platform-length strip lighting will spread an even light along the platforms.

'Noise will be cut down with platform height noise abaters on the track side of the stations.

'Wires and cables will be out of sight above a false ceiling of stainless steel slats, which will extend over the platform as far as the track.

"They will be easier to get at and we won't have to suspend services when they have to be cleaned or repaired," said Professor Black.'

From this time on the complexity of Misha Black's life is perhaps best reflected in Design Research Unit's monthly news bulletins. In the first three weeks of May, 1964, Misha Black went to Eastbourne to speak to the Furniture Industry Research Association; to Manchester to give an address when the Duke of Edinburgh presented the year's design awards; to Montreal to talk to the organisers of the Montreal 1967 World's Fair: and to Chipping Campden to speak at the SIA weekend conference on design for capital goods.

Articles published included 'The Designing Day' which appeared in *Punch* and 'Education for Industrial Design' (a paper given in Moscow in 1964 and in Prague in 1965).

This visit to Russia was not Misha Black's first return to Russia since he had left it at the age of 18 months. This had taken place in May, 1961, when he wrote *Black saw Red*, a Russian diary.

Tuesday 16 May

'On board Aeroflot Turbojet 104A. Exterior a gleaming immaculate magnificence, too impressive to be harmed by nondescript livery. Casually unshepherded up the stairs into a lofty parlour. Standard aircraft seats. For luggage, racks of polished brass and copper strong enough to hold a man, and suspended nylon nets. Trim of aluminium finished to emulate figured walnut – very high gloss. Oval centre lights, perspex in brass clips like Edwardian alabaster.

'No individual ventilation inlets. Trailing rubber tubes for emergency oxygen – a reminder of hospitals. All details cheap and elementary. But a sense of ample space. Friendly frowsy hostess who announced she was Helen. Galley midships like a country kitchen. Lavatory wash basin large enough to bath the baby. Lunch an hour late, but then with caviar and a spoon to eat it with.

Tuesday 16 May. Evening

'Airport commonplace embellished with baronial light fittings. New customs hall a workmanlike glazed shed. Formalities simple and friendly but time consuming: 60 minutes from plane touch-down to taxi take-off.

'For enquiries press a button; face appears on television screen, ask question, face answers. Very efficient.

'Leningradskya Hotel one of two post war monsters. Outside a smaller version of Moscow University. Inside soaring Victorian Venetian renaissance; marble stairs, marble columns. De luxe bedroom level of British 2nd class provincial commercial traveller's hotel, but larger. Bathroom an abattoir but spotlessly clean; all plumbing works.

Wednesday 17 May

'British Exhibition in Sokolniki Park well on way to completion. First impression: a pre-war BIF. Many stands professionally expert, but packed tight. The Russians will probably like it. They want to see *things* to compare their products with those of other countries. The recent American exhibition criticised for being too "cultural", too concerned with propaganda for a way of life which has little relation to immediate Russian possibilities.

'The town dour. The main streets so wide that the buildings lose scale. The new towers of the university, two hotels and a Government office all visually related. From the distance these stepped towers fit the scene; close to, there is no point of contact with British architectural taste. Eighteenth century stucco buildings unify the city; wooden bulidings occasionally remain; village sturdiness.

'The new architectural spirit apparent only in buildings devoid of all decoration, all quality and all character. Perhaps a purge to provide a base for new development.

'The British Embassy, a 19th century merchant's house. Magnificently placed across the river facing the Kremlin. Inside dark patinated panelling. New chairs and lamps; additions from the "Design Centre"; pleasant in themselves but too domestic for this dark serious opulence. A welcome brightness nevertheless; a shaft of the present into the British Embassy tradition. All staff efficient, pleasant and helpful; a warm patriotic glow.

'First glance of the Red Square. Not as large as in the photographs, yet inspiring in its monumental informality. A space never to be forgotten. St Basil a disappointment; its restoration in 1924 apparent. The onion domes within the Kremlin walls gleam pure gold.

'A few neon signs over restaurants and shops. An odd board for theatre and cinema posters. Sky signs on some buildings in centre; bare neon tubes advertising theatre, airways, savings. Otherwise a city without advertisement. Not a noticeable difference in city centre but a new clarity in the suburbs and roads out.

'GUM – claims to be the largest department store in the world. Could well be. Glass barrel domed conservatories each 1000 ft long – or more. Shops off each side, upper storey galleries with cross walks, more individual shops off. Milling crowds on both levels like a constructivist stage set. More space than merchandise but seemingly enough of that. Queues only for goods in short supply suddenly available. Iridescent pink expanded plastic is a popular buy on our visit. Nothing up to Western Europe standards of quality. Food shops agreeable and stocked. No more crowded than in Britain and more room to move around.

'Packaging primitive, poor paper, mediocre design. But occasionally a sophisticated pack, efficiently printed; a harbinger. Prices about as in England with an occasional joker; a small bar of chocolate for 8s.

Thursday 18 May

'Back to the British Exhibition, cantering smoothly to an easy finish. New exhibition buildings by Jack Howe compare well with those left by the Americans: two great glass boxes interconnected by bridge over road. Interior of the new buildings less crowded; good trade fair standard.

'A first meeting with Russian Expert in Industrial Design to State Committee for Co-ordination of Scientific Research. Common ground; problems identical to Britain but a later start and further to go.

'Prissy Intourist guide when needed (which is most of the time) but visitors free to move around Moscow as in any other city. The over-whelming impression of cleanliness. Not a bus ticket or cigarette carton to be seen. Streets swept, urns for waste paper and cigarette ends proliferate. Soon get into the habit of civilised tidiness. The metro spotless. Baroque grand-eur a matter for Russian taste; chandeliers and marble in the underground a symbol of national achievement.

'The Puppet Theatre. Superb technique with 3 ft figures seemingly made of sorbo rub-ber. The story "Genesis" not helped by human actors disguised as God and arch-angels.

'No bar in theatre but Russians enthusiastic drinkers of aerated syrup – like thin Coca-Cola. Self service in streets from new machines. Glass tumbler provided, washing spray and tumbler then filled with water for 1 kopek (1d) or with syrup and soda for 3 kopeks. Glass apparently not stolen or broken. These automatic machines undistin-guished in design. Each isolated object although usually grouped in banks of 3 to 6.

'The Russian automobiles comparable. Decent enough but without personality, a cross between American and British, biased towards GB. In hotel lounge leaders of British industry reading *The Daily Worker* – the only English newspaper on sale.

Friday 19 May

'To the exhibition for the last time. All finished and in good order. Congratulations for a showing of British organisational effi-ciency. The familiar vans of the British con-tractors emblazoned with "en route to Moscow" and their names in Russian made a brave sight.

'Krushchev and Ministers at opening.

'Queues for tickets, the stands thronged with Russians. Even my clients (a British bank) besieged – main interest an aerial view of London. Good-will swirling around the British even if our guide was quick to point out that everything from artificial heart to domestic refrigerator already had its Russian made equivalent.

'Sight-seeing. The Kremlin, a walled city of 80 acres. Four churches placed with perfect inconsequential relationship. The Orushezhanaya Palace: the riches of Araby, an incrustation of jewels. Russian visitors from the farms in attentive groups peer with mild surprise at their heritage from Czarist autocracy.

'I talked to 40 Russian industrialists about industrial design. The same question as in Birmingham or Manchester, scepticism about cost and value, but an intense taking of notes. Not a word missed, figures cross-checked.

'Preliminary enquiries about a British design exhibition in Moscow to better the Finnish show there last year.

'Visited the Exhibition of "Art in Everyday Life". Declined offers to be guided being full of forebodings (after three days at the Lenin-gradskya hotel) of what the Russians would exhibit and how truth could be equated with politeness. But what a surprise. The exhibi-tion elegantly presented. Very economic and simple but would not have discredited any skilled British exhibition designer. Some 7500 sq ft of exhibits in the Czar's stables. Early days yet, but a brave attempt to find contemporary design solutions – a start. Some tradition based craft work completely satisfying, all modern furniture and room settings derivative, lacking invention and quality but nevertheless a decisive step from the plush Soviet parlour.

'A last walk round Moscow. The spring much later, to my ignorant surprise, trees still thin with film of opening leaves, in odd corners small gardens protected by low fences of wood slats, these, for me, an evocation of the whole of 19th century Russia, the small clean and brushed sitting room in the street.

'Back to the Kremlin. Building of the Secretariat, saffron yellow framed in white, topping the burnt red walls of the 15th century.

'Women labourers on road work; the roads themselves needed more than their energetic hard labour, taxis plentiful and cheap. Food magnificent at beginning and end, the caviar and ice cream, but commonplace at the meal's centre.

'Finale: a quick visit to the Exhibitions of Achievements. Originally the great Agricultural exhibition of 1938. Some 500 acres of grounds, pavilions of the Soviet states; general impression that of the Paris International exhibition of 1900. Display simple and straightforward. Products on tables, captions hand lettered. But the science pavilion showed this unsophisticated display to be one facet only of the Soviet rock. Here computers to equal the British, rockets and satellites, typewriters and electronic equipment as well designed as the new pleasure ships on the river Moscwa.

'Dinner at one of the large packed Moscow restaurants, dancing energetic Western style.'

He went on to Leningrad and kept a similar diary: a very English diary. Nowhere is there expressed any race memory or emotional sympathy with things Russian. There seemed to be no difficulty about his return to his country of origin – which must have had its sense of irony, though Misha did not say so.

Rationalisation 1964–1977

'The Designing Day' gives an amusing account of Misha Black's life in England at this time. 'Boy' and 'wife' were his son Oliver and wife Joan.

'It was programmed. Already he could visualise his day as the neat small lettering in his diary, so tightly planned as to leave no time for the inevitable usurper who would arise, unbidden, to disturb that meticulous order. By the time his razor was working upwards at the stubborn chin hairs, he was convinced this was no way to organise his life, that he should eschew all planning and just get on with the job immediately to hand.

'But consciousness was seeping through to shatter the practicality of agreeable single-mindedness. The aircraft seat he was designing was suspended over his head, a board room table jostling for attention, a hospital bed was crying plaintively for action, a saucepan was lid-less awaiting his design decision, and the hotel restaurant still refused to set into an acceptable solution although the contractors were breathing down his neck for final instruction.

'His morning mockery of a swinging of arms and a kicking of legs as an analogue for

Plastic egg cup for Godfrey Holmes Ltd designed by Misha Black in 1968. This egg cup is designed to stack for easy packing and economy of space on a kitchen shelf.

exercise, and then the breathing-in which made his middle-aged stomach disappear into his backbone to create an illusion of youthful virility. Getting on – the worst of the day nearly over. But what suit does an industrial designer wear? Awkward today, neither completely a client-encountering day, nor only a working day, nor an eight-hour academic day. New dark suit for clients, the old shiny one for working, tweed for students; but what simultaneously for all three?

'His designer's experience swung into play. Most designing is the reconciliation of conflicting desiderata, so this dressy problem could easily be resolved even if as unsatisfactorily as every compromise solution. Dark suit essential to satisfy the cloakroom attendant at the client lunch now only four stomach hours away, add a grey shirt to subdue its smartness and the most ambiguous of ties. Neat but not gaudy, it will make the client happy by his whiter starched glamour and not seem ostentatious (he hoped) amongst his tweed-jacketed teaching colleagues.

'A designer, like boy scout, doctor or milkman, is always cheerful. But this morning needed no character acting. He was ahead of time, no friends in the obituary column, no newspaper report of competitors' greater successes, so he could savour his toast, kisses all round the family and he was off.

'The auguries were beatific. The sun was shining, a taxi was cruising and the driver answered with a smile instead of a snarl. Arrived, taxi paid, office door swung open. Straighten the hall chair, put the ash bin in its proper place, rub a mark off the lift button plate, slip past reception, open the door of his room. Safe – no one had intercepted him with the need for urgent decision. Fuss around the room tidying up after the chair-moving, paper-scattering cheaners. Put the

clock right, light cigarette, put diary on desk; the day has dawned.

'He used to wonder whether his carefully nurtured seeing eye was worth the effort of its cultivation. Whether it would not be easier to walk blinkered through life and be saved the anguish of always seeing the fluff on his office carpet, the eternal dust on the Venetian blinds, the chair-rubbed wall marks and the light fitting always askew. But he had decided long ago that clear sight was the designer's occupational disease, as virulent as musician's ear, athlete's foot or mother love. If the penalty for this endemic mescalin vision was the need to become a secret tidier (with his private duster and feather flick in the bottom drawer) that was compensated by sometimes getting visual pleasure from a door handle or a neat joint or an elegant sign which remained invisible to those who could only see cathedrals and sunsets.

'He was ready for work but too curious about the post to await his secretary's arrival. This was his morning's lucky dip which still remained a fascination after 30 years. The tantalisation of uncertainty was the reward for the insecurity of private practice. Anything might be lurking in those bland white corner-stamped rectangles, a new job, an old client appealing plaintively for action, an invitation to lecture or a demand for payment, the promise of an overseas journey or the necessity for a provincial visit.

'As usual the post denied its promise, no disasters and no excitements. A few notes scribbled, some replies dictated and now nothing remained to excuse him from starting work.

'When he had been younger, and hungrier, he had had a drawing board and the use of tools and the soothing pleasure of drawing out the design, slowly exploring its intricacies and experiencing the exhilarating pleasure of finding that his pen had unearthed the solution without conscious effort. But now he was too successful to be allowed such crafty pleasures. He had sprouted assistants as octopusses grow feelers and dry rot multiplies. Now he designed on backs of envelopes, on agenda papers at meetings, in taxis and on train journeys with the train's motion a hysterical adjunct to inspiration.

'He checked his diary and groaned. The first meeting was with Edward and Thomas. The furniture they were working on was an interesting enough project, but E and T were fresh scrubbed from school, cosy with their £1000 each a year, quite remorseless in their conviction that they alone amongst all humanity know what a board-room table should look like. If only they were not so able and intelligent and hard working, but there was, he knew, nothing wrong with them excepting the hardly disguised scorn with which they confronted their employer.

'The morning progressed, he had meekly exposed the sketch he had produced during yesterday's meeting of a design committee, braved the cold scorn with which E and T surveyed it as though the dog might have brought in better, thankfully stopped for office tea and closed the meeting battered but not completely bowed. Neither his nor E's nor T's concepts had survived unaltered, but the result was, he ruefully admitted, better than his original idea.

'To get any work done in the office required a special technique which he had carefully evolved. His secretary was a gentle sieve through which only the most imperative outside world penetrated – clients sieved through, contractors, colleagues, casual callers and canvassers sieve-caught. For the office interceptors the backs-to-door worked

wonders. He had arranged the table so that he, and his assistants, worked with solid backs to the door: only a crisis could make an intruder bold enough to sidle round those aggressive invader-repelling posteriors. Partners retreated quietly, only the accountant is sufficiently urgently anxious to disturb this daily repeated warfare for undisturbed working time.

'Wash and brush, dust shoes, coat on, walk across park, the serene smile adjusted, and he is ready for the client business lunch. As unflapped as his client, stories for exchange, chatter and prattle until both decide that the charade is played out and they might as well discuss the real reason for their meeting. Some gentle sparring, a fee casually dropped into the pool of coffee cups, and another commission provisionally agreed. Is this his moonstone day, or will he receive a cold reception when he tells his business manager what he has undertaken to do for a fee which only the salmon-and-Chablis-induced euphoria could have made seem momentarily reasonable?

'See an exhibition in ten minutes dead (contact with the fine arts must be maintained) and back to the office, a quick stomach-soothing Alka-Seltzer and apologies for being late for the next design meeting. A new railway coach this time. Now he is working with colleagues who have relinquished youth for maturity. They work together in complete harmony the forms grow, the materials are decided, the colours provisionally agreed. But two hours' peace is the maximum allowance, and that must be punctured by the essential telephone conversations with sweet reasonableness disguising anguished irritation. Nine hours gone, three and a half remain before dinner.

'The visiting fireman cheerfully received, cup of tea, international talk, hand over to colleague for the office tour. A dash to the school, academic look replaces the professional. A queue. A student who wants to prove that his invention warrants being patented, another who seeks his permission to marry, a meeting with his staff to plan the next series of student projects, rapid dictation, the promise to lecture tomorrow and back to the office. The designer and taxi driver in close association, the cabby drives, the designer thinks or lapses into energy-resuscitating idleness.

'The last hour. The office has unwound. Most of the staff have gone home, an artist to see about a mural to be commissioned, a colleague stayed late to settle the colour of the mosaic on a new building, the partners stroll in for an evening drink (pub hours strictly observed), minor policy decisions made, the cleaners clatter in. No time left for letter signing, dump all the papers into a briefcase, pick up a roll of drawings and back to the taxi rank.

'Through the front door into the quiet pool of home. Boy talk, wife talk, the day relived, dinner, coffee, one eye on the telly, one on letters, memoranda, notes for action tomorrow. Diary out again like a neat conscience, the next day solidifies into reality. For the last

JOHN MALTBY/DRU

General Manager's office, The Chase Manhattan Bank, Woolgate House, London EC2. Interior design, Misha Black, 1965.

half hour the still unresolved problem of the hotel restaurant creeps round to be remembered, sorted out and taken to bed. Perhaps by the morning it will be miraculously resolved.

'Shut the briefcase, glance at a technical magazine, remember that tomorrow will be an easy day: three hours to Manchester, write a report on the train, three hours inspecting a prototype machine, back and out for the evening. Sit quietly for half an hour. "What are you doing?" "I'm working".'

In 1964 also Misha Black was appointed consultant to Stewart & Morrison Ltd of Canada. This widened DRU's scope, which had already stretched to Newcastle and was later to reach Hong Kong.

Once again the brief entries in Design Research Unit's newsletters to their staff give us a glimpse of the pace and variety of the working life Misha was living at this time.

Misha Black talking to South Wales Switchgear Executives, August, 1964.

April 1965	MB to Cardiff with Lord Snowdon to the College of Advanced Technology.
7 – 10 May 1965	MB to Paris for ICSID meeting.
18 – 23 May 1965	MB to Toronto on DRU business.
16 – 19 September 1965	MB to Ulm for the second ICSID Seminar on Education of Industrial Designers.
19 – 26 September 1965	MB to Vienna for the fourth ICSID Congress.
18 October 1965	MB to Prague to lecture in connection with the Council of Industrial Design Exhibition opened by Lord Snowdon.
25 October 1965	MB to Luxembourg to take the chair at one of the sessions at the second Steel Utilisation Conference.
7 – 16 November 1965	MB to Toronto and Montreal on DRU business.

December 1965	MB elected Vice President of the Modular Society.
January 1966	MB to Brighton to lecture at the University of Sussex.
13 – 22 February 1966	MB to Budapest with a British Design Exhibition arranged by the Central Office of Information and the Council of Industrial Design in conjunction with the Hungarian Cultural Relations Office.
April 1966	MB invited to serve on the

JOHN MALTBY/DRU

Fibreglass pocket sub-station for service in the 11000/430–250 volt range. Commissioned by the South Wales Switchgear Ltd for supply to the South Western Electricity Board. Designed by Misha Black, John D. Cochrane MSIA DAEdin and Brian Cooper (logotype). 1966.

	Advisory Council of the Science Museum.
18 May 1966	MB to Humburg to judge an international competition for a city bus.
22 May 1966	MB to Canada in connection with Expo '67.

Work in this year included a pocket sub-station for South Wales Switchgear Ltd.

Design Research Unit designed not only a whole range of these sub-stations but also their enclosures, avoiding the usual unsightly barricades of netting wire.

In 1967, Misha Black was offered and accepted Honorary Fellowship of the Incorporated Institute of British Decorators and Interior Designers and was made an Honorary Vice President of the National Union of Students.

The Queen opened the small mammal house at the London Zoo, which has remained a unique interpretation of animal environment, attractive and practical in making the animals easy to see.

Misha went again behind the Iron Curtain, to Yugoslavia visiting Zagreb and Ljubljana where he held symposiums on industrial design. These meetings encouraged a sense of international cordiality. Design is a good ambassador. Nobody feels like throwing bombs when the argument is about creating visual harmony.

(Opposite above) The Charles Clore Pavilion for Small Mammals at the London Zoo, Regents Park. The photograph shows one of the three outdoor courts – this one is for wallabies and hares. In bad weather the animals have access to an enclosed den within the building where they can also be seen by the public through a window.

Dark walkways were designed to focus attention on the natural day-lighting of the cages. Splayed glass minimizes the reflection and dirtying.

(Above) 132 kV packaged substation in Kowloon, Hong Kong, supplied for the China Light and Power Company by South Wales Switchgear Ltd. Design Research Unit, 1970.

The following year, 1968, marked Design Research Unit's Jubilee, and John and Avril Blake were commissioned to write a book about the group and about the state of design in Britain at that time. The book was called *The Practical Idealists,* and was published by Lund Humphries in the following year, 1969.

Part of the book discussed the growing concern among engineers with the development of engineering design and its relationship with industrial design. The report of the Fielden Committee published in 1963 had highlighted the shortcomings in the practice of engineering design in Britain and in the education of engineering design in Britain. The Council of Industrial Design responded to the criticisms establishing a new awards scheme for capital goods in 1956 and initiating a series of conferences and exhibitions dealing with a variety of engineering design subjects and leading, in 1972, to the establishment of a new brief by government to develop and promote engineering design alongside its traditional work in industrial design.

Throughout this period, and, indeed, before the Fielden Report was published, Misha Black had become increasingly concerned with the relationship between industrial and engineering design. The overlap between the two disciplines was important to the work of DRU but was of special interest to his educational work in industrial design at the Royal Collge of Art.

As early as 1959, speaking at a conference on 'Industrial Design and the Engineering Industries' at Birmingham, he had said:

' ... the industrial designer, by training, concentration of interest and personality, differs in important aspects from the engineer. If the industrial designer is properly assimilated within the design team, then these very differences become the flint against which the steel of the engineer can strike more imaginative blows.

'In the past, over-generalization has again led to unnecessary argument about whether or not the industrial designer should be part of the engineering design team. In fact this should depend on the importance of human values in the particular product concerned. The use a medical analogy, if you have a headache you can probably cure it yourself, by taking a couple of aspirins; but if you break a leg it would be wise to go to a doctor. Similarly, simple ergonomic problems can often be handled by an industrial designer or engineer by reference to appropriate data in the text-books, but if it is a complex or unfamiliar problem, requiring fresh experimental research, then the sensible approach would be to go to a trained ergonomist. In the same way a person with four or five years' training in industrial design is likely to make a better job of the appearance and user factors in a product where these are important to his success. Where they are not, then designers skilled in other specialised areas should be able to deal, themselves, with the minor headaches of human values.

'What emerges from this proposition is the concept of a body of professional people held together by the common discipline of design; but they will be designers working in a variety of specialised fields, some concerned with structures, some with plastics, some with circuitry, some with ergonomics, some with graphics, and so on. The degree of specialisation will vary and there will certainly be a need, on the one hand, for highly specialised designers and, on the other, for co-ordinating designers of wide experience. Within the context the term "industrial designer", referring as it does to only one group of specialists, is highly misleading, for all the specialised designers we have referred to are working for industry.

'We have explained in the first chapter the peculiar origins of the term "industrial design"; after 50 years of use and 25 years of Government promotion of the activity it represents, it will be difficult to get rid of. Yet it may have done immeasurable harm to the more rapid acceptance of a unified philosophy of design.

'It would be far better if some other term, which frankly acknowledged the industrial designer's preoccupation with aesthetics and human values, could be found.'

Later in 1972, writing on "Engineering and Industrial Design" he went on to say:

'The use of a generic term to define a specific activity is a source of irritation to those who, participating in the total operation, are affronted by the presumption of a smaller group who purloin the title for a minor specialisation. "Industrial design" is a generic term of this kind and there is little reason for its use in the restrictive manner which has now gained world-wide recognition, in spite of justified objections from engineers who rightly claim that much of their work is "industrial design" if these words mean, as they clearly do, design for industrial production.

'Nevertheless "industrial design" has, over the past 45 years, assumed a discrete connotation. It is used throughout the world to describe a branch of engineering as specific as a specialisation in electrical, mechanical or structural engineering. In Italy it is *disegno industriale*, in Spain and Argentina *deseno industrial,* in German *Formgebung,* while in the USA, Japan, Israel, Canada, Sweden and elsewhere the English version is a recognised description.

'For a time at the Royal College of Art in London an attempt was made to achieve a more precise description by naming the department concerned the "School of Industrial Design (Engineering)" to differentiate its discipline from those of the Schools of Furniture, Ceramics and Textile design which are equally concerned with designing for industry: but now the RCA has succumbed to international pressure and has dropped the bracketed "engineering".

'The term has now achieved international usage, but a precise definition of the function its purports to describe eludes even its most experienced practitioners. Clearly it is not intended to describe the activity of designers in the ancient but extant craft-based industries in which, although handicraft has been largely superseded by automated processes, explanation is needed of the function of a textile designer, the ceramics designer, or designers in the furniture, jewellery or fashion industries. In these trades, and in the technologies which support them, the need for designers who equate technical knowledge with creativity is established; the engineer provides the machines, the designer decides what they shall produce. There is a close relationship between the development of new materials, manufacturing techniques and the design of the consumer products which they facilitate, but it remains true that the shape and surface pattern of domestic ceramics and the form of glass and cutlery are prime motivators of the desire to own and use, and decisions which govern these aspects of domestic products are the undisputed responsibility of the artist/designer.

'Industrial design, in the present meaning of this term, is, however, only marginally concerned with the industries based on the ancient crafts; industrial designer are involved in the design of refrigerators and washing machines, typewriters and compu-

ters, automobiles and locomotives, telephone instruments and microscopes, medical equipment and machine tools – with the whole cornucopia of the light and heavy engineering industries. These are fields of design in which mechanical engineers have functioned to their own satisfaction for many decades and it is not surprising that they question the need for a further specialisation to be added to their skills.

'The profession of industrial design is rooted in a relatively distant past, distorted by recent injections. Its roots are in the arts and crafts movement of the second half of the 19th century when William Morris wrote "What business have we at all with art unless all can share it?" But its ethical and philosophical intention was knocked askew by the Victorian industrialists who looked only for profit from design and founded art schools to train "art technicians". The fine art concept of industrial design received its body blow in the late 1920s and early 1930s when the then young emergent American designers such as Harold Van Doren, Raymond Loewy, Henry Dreyfuss, Walter Dorwin Teague and Norman Bel Geddes proved conclusively that re-design could imbue products with and aura of the immediate present which encouraged sales. Since the 1930s the industrial designers and their well wishers and critics have balanced uneasily between a conviction that their duty is to support the tenets of William Morris and combine beauty with utility, and pressures to follow the credo of Raymond Loewy and see beauty only in the upward sweep of the line on a sales graph.

'I mention these crudely opposing views only because critical and theoretical argument is still often polarised at these oversimplified extremes. The industrial designers themselves tend to deal more pragmatically with the tasks which face them, with finding solutions to immediate problems, but confusion as to the meaning and intention of industrial design persists ...'

Education for design

'If industrial design can be distinguished as a separate discipline from that of mechanical engineering (however closely related they may be) one would expect the divergencies to be exemplified by the education which feeds each profession. This is clearly the case. Education for a primary engineering degree is still largely based on intense specialisation with engineering science as the core subject. Only recently has engineering design as such begun to gain academic respectability. The concept that social studies can usefully be associated with engineering remains a novelty although it is now gaining credence at some universities.

'At Imperial College 10 per cent to 15 per cent of students' degree credits may optionally be garnered from studies in "The Sociology of Innovation", "Environment and Man", and so on. Lectures are available in literature, architecture, economics, poetry and politics. At Cambridge students may, in the final of their first degree years, study "Statistics and Operational Research", "The Sociology of Organisations" and economics. At the University of Sussex social studies account for one ninth of the curriculum, and a degree may be taken in "Engineering with Social Studies" in which the latter subject occupies a third of the course.

'I believe that these moves, and equivalent ones at other universities and polytechnics, towards liberalising engineering education go some way towards releasing the young engineer from the contraints of over-specialisation and allow for the development of personality and human understanding which are essential if inherent creativity is to be released.

'More has been done in some American universities where attempts are being made to formulate engineering curricula which include the cultivation of creativity as a major objective. This attitude has been summarised by Dr William Bollay, Visiting Professor at Stanford University. He writes: "The inventive ability is a human characteristic like the musical and artistic ability. It is not possible by education to produce a great inventor or innovator if the student did not have any initial talent in this direction. On the other hand the creative ability can be nurtured and improved or developed by example and encouragement and constant practice. It can also be suppressed and discouraged by disuse, by keeping a student so busy learning facts and methods of analysis that he does not have any opportunity to exercise his inventive talent.

"I do not wish to encourage a dilettante attitude to mechanical engineering. Detailed knowledge and experience of the disciplines of the subject are crucial to effective professional practice, but the need now is to loosen the constraints of factual accumulation and analytical methods to enable young engineers to synthesise as well as analyse, create as well as efficiently follow known precepts.

"The academic air is full of talk about divergent thinking, random juxtaposition and the displacement of concepts; as engineering educators begin to attach importance to these concepts so they make it possible for the students in their charge to release the creative capacities on which Britain's existence as an industrialised society depends – and this it must be if we are to retain a level of industrial production which will allow us to improve our own standards of living and social welfare and make a more realistic contribution towards helping the third world to match even our present level of nutrition, housing and social services ...

"At present the industrial designer is, and should be, an assertive collaborator. In the words of the editor of *Engineering:* 'Industrial designers have already achieved a quality of design and workmanship which must command the respect of engineers as it already commands the respect of the consumers and the community.'

"Engineers, by virtue of their education and training, tend to start with the mechanics or their design, whereas industrial designers tend to start with the end use of the end user, whether it is the consumer or the community. While they may be debarred from a good deal of engineering design because of their limited engineering knowledge, nevertheless they have something valuable to contribute because of their unique starting point in design. There is room for both kinds of designers – engineers and industrial designers. And the most advanced firms are already making use of the two disciplines and marrying them successfully for the benefit of their sales.

"This describes a reasonable situation and provides the soothing balm of respectability for which those of my generation who battled for many decades against entrenched and vigorous opposition to industrial design are grateful. The influence of the industrial designer may extend in a factory beyond his engineering tasks. His knowledge of colour and form and their emotive effects makes him a useful consultant on environmental problems in workshops, offices and social welfare accommodation: his experience in typography acts as a link between the engineering design office and those responsible for technical literature and instruction information. If he has been effectively educated and is allowed the proper status in the industrial hierarchy he can be a link man between many sectors of the workshops, drawing offices, research laboratory and management which too often are still surounded by constricting walls of unrelieved specialisation. He can bridge science, industry, commerce and art, be able to talk, with enthusiasm and with at least a modicum of knowledge, about contemporary movements in the arts, as he can be enthusiastic about new materials, technological innovation and sales campaigns.

"This is all to the good, and within this job specification the need is for more facilities for the education of industrial designers, for their being employed in larger numbers by British industry and allowed the opportunity to use their special capabilities and skills to the maximum extent.

"But this, I believe, is only the first stage towards the effective use of the amalgam of talent, knowledge and experience which we categorise as industrial design. It is clear that Britain must regain an urgent creativity if it is to re-establish world supremacy in engineering design. Papers and committee reports on the need for improved standards in engineering design have proliferated over the past quarter century but the products of our engineering industries have rarely equalled the criteria of those who proclaim them. There is no single or simple answer to this problem which needs the totality of creative imagination and technical ability in this country for its solution. In this battle for survival, and it is clearly no less if we are not content to become a picturesque archeological backwater, different attitudes are needed from those which fashioned British industry in the later 19th and early 20th century.

"Among the techniques which should be developed is, I believe, the use of industrial designers, but in a different way from that which I have previously described. If the willingness to employ them existed, I would like to see the colleges of art and design produce designers whose technical knowledge might be limited but whose generalised creative ability had been developed to a tight-wire tautness. They would be basically artists with a strongly developed sense of social responsibility and an intense interest in science and technology – irritants in the development team rather than well-mannered diplomatic collaborators.

This is not entirely a fanciful conception; creativity is not born of well-intentioned honest work; it needs to be fired by enthusiasm and annealed in the clash of conflicting personalities. I am not suggesting that our factories should be infested by a rabble of artists, but I believe that, in the long term, the injection of untamed creativity (in small doses) might induce the convulsive spasm which some bed-ridden aspects of our industry require.

"The education of artist/designers who are intended to be catalysts rather than practical executants would represent pedagogic problems, but I believe sufficient experimental work has been done in some educational institutions throughout the world to make this a practical possibility. The course would still need to be based on engineering technology as architecture is based on the technology of the building industry, but it would ally technology with art, poetry with practicality. It would require five years of carefully planned study, although the plan might need to be implied rather than prescribed, but it could produce a few more engineers possessed by vital creativity.

"In the meanwhile, however, I am content with the growing acceptance of industrial designers as specialised technicians adding their skills to those of the other equally specialised engineers in design development teams. The results of this collaboration have already been impressive and nationally important – it is now necessary quickly to expand from its well established base."'

In 1968 Misha Black was asked to design new offices for the Alliance Building Society in Hove, and he had lunch with the Queen at Buckingham Palace. He went to Milan for the Triennale and Venice for the Biennale. He discussed the Victoria Line during the BBC's 'Ten o'Clock' television programme.

In 1969 he was made design consultant for Woolgate House in the City of London. He accepted an invitation to become a member of the Cultural Advisory Committee of the United Kingdom National Commission for UNESCO and he was present when the Queen opened the Victoria Line at Green Park Station on 7 March.

In 1970 he went on a lecture tour of Australia at the invitation of the Industrial Design Council of Australia. He talked about 'A Survey of Industrial Design in the Engineering Industries'; 'Craftsmen and Designers'; 'Education of the Industrial Designer' and 'The Creation of Environment'.

In 1970 Misha Black was also elected a companion of the Institution of Mechanical Engineers. He went to Barcelona as a member of the jury judging ADI/FAD Design Awards and to Killarney for a seminar on design education sponsored by the Department of Education and the Irish Export Board.

In January, 1971, he went to India to talk about the development of their engineering and industrial design education. Here he was careful to clear confusion between the terms 'industrial design' and 'design engineering' and went on to talk about logic and creativity:

Joan and Misha Black at home, September 1970.

'I believe that logic requires creativity, that logical solutions are not only a question of mathematical addition, that to carry a logical problem through to a conclusion itself can be, but not always is, a creative process.'

In 1972 he went on a trip to to Hong Kong on behalf of the British Council. His many achievements were recognisd in this year when he was also awarded a knighthood, bestowed on him by the Queen on 12 July.

MONITOR PRESS FEATURES LTD

Oliver, Joan, Misha and Julia Black, 1972, on the day when Misha Black was made a Knight Bachelor of the British Empire.

'So I trollied bales of silk to East End dressmakers and sold made-to-measure enamelled table tops to hygienic housewives ....'

It had been a long way for Cinderella and he had had to be his own Prince Charming. It was a far cry, too, from the boy who had wanted to be an ARTIST. He still produced the occasional drawing, but it was his written work and lecturing that meant most to the many colleagues who were his audience. His written work in this year included 'The History of the International Council of Industrial Design' published in the Japanese *Industrial Art News*. Also 'Personal Failure' for ARK magazine in which, at the end of all he had achieved, he was to say

> ' ... I take irresponsible consolation in the knowledge that what I have designed is my personal graffito and that jobs still to be done will occupy my time until the final personal failure of death itself.'

In November, 1973, Misha Black was elected Master of the Faculty of Royal Designers for Industry for 1973/74. He was also made President of the Design and Industries Association. Recognition in this way by fellow designers meant a great deal to him.

In December, 1973, he gave an after lunch talk to the Wynken de Worde Society on 'The Unity of Design'. In this he said that unity of design was

> 'an attitude of mind transmuted by technical proficiency whether the problem be the design of a title page of a book or of an automobile, the design of a stamp or of a hospital bed...
>
> 'Even if the design objective is only to give momentary pleasure, its value should not be disregarded.'

On 28 March, 1974, Misha gave a talk with slides to the IES National Lighting Conference on 'National Design'. The following day, as President of the Design and Industries Association, he attended a seminar in Amsterdam on the subject of rubbish disposal. In the same month, Joan and Misha Black won first prizes at a Royal College of Art masked party by wearing masks designed by Sue Allnut of Design Research Unit.

In 1975, Sir Misha Black retired as Professor of Industrial Design to the Royal College of Art and his place was filled by Frank Height. Addressing the Court, Sir Misha said:

> 'Mr Provost and Members of the Court,
>
> 'When I started to work at the RCA (if such a pleasure can be so described) I approached my room in the Western Galleries past the legs of a man dangling from a kite. This daily glimpse of the infancy of aeronautics was an appropriate reminder of the possiblities of technological development. It encouraged me to believe that we could advance from a situation in which I knew nothing about education, while my students matched my ignorance. Over the past 15 years we have, in the School of Industrial Design, stridden from kites to aircraft, and while we may not yet be jet propelled we have at least got our feet into the aircraft although happily not always on the ground.
>
> 'I had, as a teacher, the advantage of not myself having received any technical education, which convinced me that creativity without technical knowledge and experience results only in superficial styling, while the essence of industrial design is not styling but style – the most rigorous and taxing of all controls on free expression.
>
> 'The technical content of our course has therefore always been our armature. There is no guarantee that a school can producer outstanding designers, but it can ensure that its graduates are professionally competent. If

this is its modest aim it may well become a springboard for the high fliers. Let me hasten to add that my certainty of the correctness of this pedagogic attitude is related to post-graduate education and I would be less enamoured of my disciplinarian stance if I were concerned with under-graduate teaching. In fact, we had some experience of this, as for seven years or so we served a direct entry of young men (and a few girls) direct from the sixth form of general education. We gave them free rein, and under two brilliant teachers, Denis Bowen and Bernard Myers, they blossomed into vigorous capability – engines generated by their own internal combustion. Their first year course did not differ greatly from that of the traditional Bauhaus foundation, but with the emphasis shifted slightly from experiment to problem-solving. The success of this experiment proved, at least to my satisfaction, that intelligent boys and girls are not polarized scientists *or* humanists but that they can illuminate each aspect of creative endeavour by a sympathy for the other. Neither have we found it incongruous for the students to spend an evening

Third year students and staff at the Royal College of Art, June 1971. Misha Black is third from the left.

drawing from life followed by a morning studying the malleable properties of aluminium.

'We sadly, however, jettisoned our younger set on the altar of university status and concentrated all our energies on the sterner stuff of DipAD, leavened by a sprinkling of engineering graduates. Our brief to these students was, and remains, deceptively simple. Industrial design, we said, and still say, is an amalgam of technical knowledge, creativity, communication, social understanding and aesthetic discrimination. I shall not bore you with details of pedagogic methods, but it is evident that technology and communicative skills can be taught but that creativity, aesthetic sensitivity and social responsibility can only be encouraged.

'Two question marks have hovered over our heads since the establishment of the School in 1959, and time has not diminished their unsettling potency. The first questions the relevance of a department of industrial design (which is an aspect of mechanical engineering) in a college of *art*; the second queries the equation of social responsibility with the design of artefacts such as automobiles, which some believe are socially malevolent.

It would certainly be more comfortable if industrial design were taught in isolation or attached to a college of technology, but the result would not satisfy my ambition for this youngest of the creative disciplines.

'I believe in intense specialisation, in growth from a core of specific knowledge and experience into wider fields of understanding and executant capacity, but I equally believe that during the initial period of specialisation the essential requirement exists of an appreciation of its wider implications. I therefore disdain academic isolation and monastic

exclusivity. Industrial design, as I understand it, is more than the capacity to determine the ergonomic requirement, form, surface, texture and colour of machine-made artefacts; it is more than a concern for the effectiveness of people within mechanical systems; it requires the acceptance of responsibility for the quality of our man-made world, and this can only be achieved, in the long run, by designers whose horizon is not limited by myopic concern for technical achievement. No designer cen reach this goal unless, during his formative period, he has been buffeted by opposing attitudes and a flat contradiction of his own standards of values. The Royal College of Art is the buffeting institution *par excellence*. No student of the College can remain indifferent to the attitudes of his contemporaries whose work questions the foundations of his own doctrine. The common facilities are shared by all students, whether they be industrial designers or painters; general studies ensure a dialectic interchange. Any student who remains unaffected by the challenge of his denigrators is destined to become a dedicated back room boy – and this is not the habitat envisaged for our graduates.

'The industrial design students who have been most often attacked as pariahs outside the bounds of RCA tolerance have been those specialising in automotive design. Their devotion to sculptured form (even if reasonably related to function) has been seen by some, including a number of their own colleagues, as pandering to the less seemly aspects of our 20th century humanity, to pride rather than honest worth. As far as the creative act is concerned, I see little difference between a passion for form related to a vehicle and an equal passion for the pattern of a textile, the shape of a garment or the form of yet another chair which fulfils a symbolic as well as a practical need. But it does raise basic issues of social responsibility; a pedestrian killed by an elegent car is still a dead pedestrian. Even magnificient machines despoil historic cities.

'While the demand exists, however, for these symbolic vehicles, some students will continue to lavish their talents on the design of motor cars to which they are as devoted as a groom to his charger, but the majority of our industrial design students now seek more overt social justification for their projects, and concentrate either on heavy engineering, where the limits for aesthetic manoeuvre are reduced, or on projects for the disabled or disadvantaged. Work of a high order of technical competence, social understanding and aesthetic discernment has been undertaken on equipment for the physically handicapped, play and self training vehicles for spina-bifida children, specialised equipment for the seriously sick and intermediate technology for developing countries. In such work compassion has been added to competence. This wave of compassionate concern has now reached a height to justify our planning a major exhibition and symposium to be held here in the Spring of 1976 where complete projects will be displayed and evaluated and a new base established for further exploration of what we are calling "The Dimensions of Design". In this venture we are supported by The Design Council, the Royal Society of Art, the Society of Industrial Artists and Designers and the Design and Industries Association, which have all willingly accepted the leadership of the RCA.'

He ended:

'The RCA today is a very different institution from what it was when I first climbed the stairs to the left of the suspended legs of the astronaut. It was good then; it is better now.

It was a splendid hierarchical institution; it is now an academic community and for this, as for so many other things, we have to thank our Rector, Lord Esher.

'This is the first and last time that I shall have the privilege of addressing the Court. At the end of the year I shall leave the College the richer for my time here, with memories which combine affection with gratitude.'

He was elected Professor Emeritus to the College.

In September, 1975, Sir Misha Black was re-appointed Chairman of the Culture Advisory Committee to the United Kingdom National Commission to UNESCO. He was also appointed a member of the jury for the Museum of the Year Award. He gave a paper at the National Conference of the Association of Art Institutions on 'Art and Design Education'.

In February of the following year he was awarded an Honorary Fellowship of the Sheffield Polytechnic. He become a member of the Committee for the environment for the Queen's Silver Jubilee Celebrations. He gave a lecture to the Institute and College of Craft Education at their Nottingham Conference on 'Craft: Art or Design?' In this he said:

'Learning about craft is as important as learning through craft.

'Craft work cannot be smudged over. There is no escape from the eyeball confrontation when what is made looks at its creator and judges him as he judges his creation.'

In this same month, February 1976, Sir Misha undertook a tour of the recently built underground systems of the Hong Kong Mass Transit Railway together with the railway's director of engineering and two Freeman Fox partners.

In May he was appointed a member of the Council of the Royal College of Art.

At the end of that month he spent two weeks in Czechosolvakia on behalf of the British Council

DRU

UNIVERSITY OF BRADFORD

Lok Fu underground station, Hong Kong Mass Transit Railways, designed by Design Research Unit, 1969.

Misha Black, second from the left, when he was made an Honorary Doctor of Technology at the University of Bradford in 1975.

under the UK/Czechoslovakian Culture Exchange Programme.

In October, 1976, Sir Misha was appointed a member of the examining board for Anglo/USA Bicentennial Awards. He was also employed as the sole expert witness in a copyright case between Agfa and Braun.

In 1977 he was involved in work for the Silver Jubilee Exhibition in Hyde Park and wrote an article 'In Praise of Plastics.'

However in the spring of this year he fell ill and had to be rushed to hospital where it was found that he had a tumour on the brain. He was operated on and, for a time, the operation seemed to have been successful. To the last, Sir Misha talked coherently with friends and looked through his mail. He died, however, on 11 August and a memorial service was held at St James's, Piccadilly, on 19 October. The Duke of Edinburgh was represented by Mr Richard Davies and the Duke of Gloucester was present.

Mr Oliver Black (Sir Misha's only son by his second marriage) read one of John Donne's holy sonnets and Lord Reilly of Brompton gave an address. Lord Reilly had, however, already written Sir Misha's obituary for *The Times*. In it he said of Misha Black:

'The qualities that made him successful as a teacher and a designer were his clear-sightedness and his ability to extract the essence from any idea: also his attention to detail. He was a good administrator with high standards, and a difficult man to please.

'As a designer he had a fund of invention which he never allowed to distract him from the central purpose of the design, a quality which also made him as useful committee member – firm though softly spoken. He was a man of notable good will, taking trouble to help many worthy causes.'

To the author, a watcher-on-the-sidelines of the emerging profession of industrial design throughout the past 30 years, Misha Black seemed to conjure miracles of something out of nothing, helping to create a whole new world with its own rules and charters, ideals and quests for truth. Design has been described as 'the creative leap,' a pure inspiration, an assessment of intangible needs made valid as business. Misha could make this conjuring seem normal and logical. Even *art* was sane.

It is too soon to see Misha Black's work in its historical context. All that is certain is that his sense of what was fashionably interesting and his ability to give this a wide perspective did win him a place in the history of design: a well respected place.

Bibliography

Blake, A. (ed) *The Black Papers*, Pergamon Press, Oxford 1983.

Blake, J. and A. *The Practical Idealists*, Lund Humphries, London 1969.

Middleton, M. *Group Practice in Design*, Architectural Press, London 1967.

Other works

Physical Planning (contributor), Architectural Press, London 1945.

The Practice of Design (contributor), Lund Humphries, London 1946.

'1851–1951' in *The Ambassador* no. 8, 1946.

Exhibition Design (ed), Architectural Press, London 1950.

'The Architects' Anguish' The Harry Peach Memorial Lecture, Leicester University, 15 November 1962.

'Amenity on the Road' talk at the Engineering For Traffic Conference, London, July 1963.

'Industrial Design and Building Services' talk at the Institute of Heating and Ventilating Engineers' Annual Conference, 1963.

'Office 2000' in *Punch*, September 1963.

'Education and Practice in Industrial Design' talk for design symposiums at Moscow and Warsaw(1964), Prague (1965), Budapest (1966) and Zagreb (1967).

'Education for Industrial Design' in *Nature* (London) no. 4926, 1964.

'Industrial Design: Art or Science?' talk to American Society of Industrial Designers, Philadelphia, USA, 17 October 1964.

Reports of ICSID/UNESCO seminars on industrial design education (ed) at Bruges (1964), Ulm (1965) and Syracuse (1967). (Now in the Misha Black archive at the Victoria & Albert Museum.)

'The Education of Industrial Designers' The Cantor Lectures, in *The Royal Society of Arts Journal* no. 5111, 1965.

'The Education of Interior Designers' in *Architectural Review*, 15 December 1965.

'Computing Design' talk to The Society of Industrial Artists and Designers, 24 Nov. 1965.

'Design: the Creation of Environment' talk at Ontario College of Art, Toronto, Canada, 8 November 1966.

'Designing for People', talk to the Institute of Directors, Manchester, 4 May 1967.

'Anti-Design' in *The Queen*, 7 July 1967.

Group Practice in Design (contributor), Architectural Press , London 1967.

Industrial Design – an International Survey (ed), UNESCO/ICSID, Brussels 1967.

'The Training of Interior Designers' in *Commercial Decor*, 4 June 1968.

'Humanising our Cities' in *The Sunday Times*, 2 February 1968.

'Theories of Industrial Design' talk at Norwegian Design Centre, Oslo, 11 February 1968.

'The Interaction of the Arts and Technology' talk at UNESCO Conference, Tbilisi, USSR, 1968.

'Transatlantic Dialogue' talk at International Design Conference, Aspen, Colorado, 1968.

'Zum Standort des Industrial Design' in *Form* no. 42/27, Kassel 1968.

The Misha Black Australian Papers, Trevor Wilson Publishing, Sydney 1970.

'The Aesthetics of Engineering' for the Institute of Mechanical Engineers, 1 Birdcage Walk, London SW1H 9JT, circa 1970.

Notes on Two Seminars of the Coldstream/ Summerson Joint Committee, 14 October 1970. (Now in the Misha Black archive.)

'Problems of Design Education' in *Export*, November 1970.

'Design in Long Range Planning' in *Long Range Planning*, Bradford 1970.

'Personal Failure' in *ARK* no. 48, Royal College of Art, London 1971.

'Notes on Design Education in Britain' in *Nature*, 5 May 1971.

'Colour in Decoration' in *Building*, 15 Nov. 1971.
'Trends in Residential Architecture' in *The Jewish Chronicle*, 23 December 1971.
'The Function of Design in Long Range Planning in *The Journal of Long Range Planning*, vol. 5, no. 2, 1972.
'The Polytechnic Scare' in *The Designer*, 3 Jan. 1972
'The Relevance of Industrial Design in 1980' talk to Selskabet for Industrial Formgivning, Copenhagen and Svenska Slodjdforeningen, Stockholm, 2 February 1972.
'Engineering and Creativity' talk to The Engineering Society of Hong Kong, 22 March 1972.
'The History of ICSID' in *Kogei News* (The Journal of the Japanese Industrial Designers' Association), vol. 40/1, June 1972.
'Disillusion of Industrial Design' in *The Times Higher Educational Supplement*, 28 July 1972.
'Engineering and Industrial Design' in *The Institution of Mechanical Engineers' Proceedings*, vol. 186, January 1973.
'Design for Europe', 12 December 1972. (Now in the Misha Black archive.)
'The Designer and Manager Syndrome' A Tiffany Lecture on Corporate Design Management, New York, 2 October 1973.
'The Unity of Design' for The Wynken de Worde Society, c/o 42 Bedford Avenue, London WC1B 3AT, March 1974.
'A View of Art and Design' talk to the Association of Art Institutions, 1974.
'The Environment of Transport' for the London Transport Executive, 55 Broadway, London SW1H 0BD, 1975.
'Is Design Any Good?' talk to the Institute of Public Relations, May 1975.
'Architecture, Art and Design in Unison' in *A Tonic to the Nation*, Thames & Hudson 1975.
'Design Needs Art' in *Design* no. 321, Sept. 1975.
'Design for Need', October 1976. (Now in the Misha Black archive.)
'Advances in Industrial Design' in *The Indian and Eastern Engineer*, 28 October 1976.
'Week by Week, 15 November 1976. (Now in the Misha Black archive.)
'The Aesthetics of Plastics' The Professor Moore Memorial Lecture, The University of Bradford, 3 March 1977.
Miscellaneous papers in Boxes 14, 15 and 16 of the Misha Black archive at the Victoria & Albert Museum.